SEX

is a

13-letter

word

Wishing you joy
in love & life

A Guide to Healthier, Happier,
More Loving Relationships

by

Carolyn Chernenkoff B.S.N.
William Chernenkoff M.D.

Co-therapists in
marital and sexual counselling

Carolyn Chernenkoff

William Chernenkoff

SEX IS A 13-LETTER WORD
by
Carolyn Chernenkoff B.S.N.
William Chernenkoff M.D.

Second Printing – May 1996

Canadian Cataloguing in Publication Data

 Chernenkoff, Carolyn, 1941-

  Sex is a 13-letter word

  ISBN 1-895292-67-0

1. Sex therapy.   2. Sex counseling.   3. Interpersonal
relations.   I. Chernenkoff, William, 1939-
I. Title.

RC557.C44 1995   306.7   C95-920212-9

Designed, Printed and Produced in Canada by
Centax Books, A Division of PrintWest Communications Ltd.
Publishing Director, Margo Embury
1150 Eighth Avenue, Regina, Saskatchewan
Canada S4R 1C9
(306) 525-2304   Fax (306) 757-2439

CRITICAL ACCLAIM

"This is an excellent, practical book for all people who are in relationships, contemplating relationships or looking back on failed relationships. It provides rich insights into common issues of sexuality and relationships in a very readable, understandable and balanced fashion. The balance arises from an equal emphasis placed on both sexual partners and models the Chernenkoff's approach in therapy."

(Dr. David Keegan – Professor of Psychiatry,
University of Saskatchewan)

"The series of dialogue interviews which were carried out with Colin Grewar, I am sure was of invaluable assistance to many who listened in to the CBC Radio broadcasts . . . and now it will be of further assistance in printed form. Their treatment of the subject of human sexuality; the direct dealing with a wide scope of situations; provides choice exposure to the reader. Highlighting their points with role playing, often humorous, provides a relaxing text. The subject matter is written with clarity and is very informative. One could easily say it is prepared by those "in the know" (Carolyn and Bill) for those who would like to know more.

(Rev. Stewart N. Dingwall – Minister, United Church of Canada)

"Like its authors, this book is witty, sometimes irreverent and always entertaining. The subject matter is discussed with sensitivity, in an easy, conversational style."

(Dr. Anne F. Doig – Clinical Assistant,
Professor of Obstetrics and Gynecology,
University of Saskatchewan)

"An excellent guide to a healthy and happy sexual relationship. A must for all to read."

(Dr. Marilyn Davidson – Clinical Associate Professor,
Department of Obstetrics and Gynecology,
University of Saskatchewan)

FOREWORD BY COLIN GREWAR

A friend of mine suggested I call this the "foreplay" rather than the "foreword." I kind of liked the idea!

We don't hear much talk about sex on the radio. Certainly not on CBC Radio and not on a provincial program that airs between 4:00 and 6:00 on weekday afternoons. My colleagues and I on *The Afternoon Edition* knew we were taking a risk when we introduced a regular column on *Sex and Relationships* to our radio audience across Saskatchewan; that there would be those who would not want to listen to discussions about premature ejaculation, faking an orgasm or love at the office while they were driving the kids to hockey practice. We were sensitive to those concerns but we went ahead with the column because we believed strongly in its relevance, in its value and possibilities and we believed in Bill and Carolyn Chernenkoff.

The idea was to talk about sex and relationships in an open, direct and positive way and to do so in a relaxed and conversational manner. After all, isn't this the way we should talk about these things? Bill and Carolyn offered us impeccable credentials, knowledge and understanding. They know what they're talking about. Collectively, they also offered us great "radio personality." As a host I couldn't ask for two more wonderful guests. They're expressive, passionate, spontaneous, anecdotal, well prepared and they're very funny. Just like any other thirty-something male I have hang-ups about sex. It's not something I talk about openly to just anyone. But with Bill and Carolyn I felt perfectly comfortable. We were always confident that the conversational quality of the columns and Bill and Carolyn's warmth and enthusiasm made the majority of our listeners comfortable as well, no matter what the topic.

What you have here is a book that consists of word-for-word transcripts of our ten-minute "on-air" discussions on sex and relationships. This format captures the spirit of Bill and Carolyn. They're better in person, but this is the next best thing! I think it also makes the book more accessible: most of us prefer a conversation to a lecture and find dialogue more engaging than monologue. Most importantly, this format reinforces the Chernenkoff's central theme: We have to talk to each other if we're going to find and sustain rich and happy relationships.

I gained a great deal of knowledge, understanding and enjoyment from each and every one of my studio sessions with Bill and Carolyn Chernenkoff. I hope this book does the same for you.

TABLE OF CONTENTS

PREFACE

Fifty percent of all couples in North America will experience some sort of marital or sexual distress or dysfunction at some time during their relationship. If you look down your street, that is every second household.

Out of that fifty percent who are experiencing distress, seventy percent can be helped with accurate factual information.

This book provides that information in a fun, easy-to-read, dialogue form which originated as programs on the *Relationships Column* on CBC Radio.

It is our hope that, for some, this information may prevent problems from developing and for others it may relieve dissatisfaction by stimulating thought and dialogue. For some the book will be just that much needed catalyst to the discussion and interaction that will relieve distress.

If the dissatisfaction in a relationship is beyond what this information can relieve, we hope this book provides comfort in the assurance that it is all right to seek professional help.

Carolyn & Bill

ACKNOWLEDGEMENTS

To Masters and Johnson, St. Louis, Missouri, for their openness in sharing their research and knowledge with all the world.

Like Panasonic, they are always "slightly ahead of their time."

Their vast knowledge and experience will be the hallmark of therapy for generations to come.

To Colin Grewar and CBC Radio who were pioneers in broadcasting topics on sexuality in a professional and positive way. It was their creative foresight that made this book possible.

INTRODUCTION

Friday mornings we would awaken with anticipation, excitement and terror. By 10:45 a.m., we had to be in the CBC Radio studio to tape two programs for the *Afternoon Edition*. The ritual was to arrive at the CBC studios, Midtown Plaza with time to spare. We would leave our home early in case of traffic jams, overturned semis or other disasters which might prevent us from arriving on time. On the way we listened to a Bette Midler tape to "pump up the adrenaline." If we did not do this, we found our interviews flat and dull.

After arriving at the plaza, we would purchase flavored coffee to go from the food court, waiting until the "exact moment" to take the coffee upstairs with us.

At 10:45, with mutual tachycardia, we would enter the CBC studios, where we were greeted warmly by receptionist, Denise, and engineering technician, Mark Behrend.

Through the marvels of modern technology, we would be connected to Colin Grewar in Regina with the usual high-tech opening remarks,

"Hello? . . . Hello? . . . Can you hear me? . . . Can you hear me now? . . ."

We sat on opposite sides of the table with our earphones and microphones. Carolyn had the chair with the view . . . she was able to look past Bill, out the window, all the way down 21st Street to the Bessborough Hotel. Beside us, in a room the size of a walk-in closet, was Mark Behrend, with all his electronic connections to Colin Grewar in Regina.

The studio, built on the site of the old CNR station, was the setting for five years of CBC Radio appearances for the *Relationships Column*. Most of the success of the *Column* belongs to Colin Grewar. Despite advance warnings by nearly everyone from CBC that "Colin would be uncomfortable with sex," we found quite the contrary. The warnings may have reflected the discomfort of the "soothsayers." Colin made us feel warm and comfortable, and "we all talked about sex as if we weren't talking about sex."

Although we had a topic or theme in mind for each show, with an outline of ideas to be covered, the programs, in fact, were all done spontaneously, without any paper in front of us. Amazingly, each program turned out "live to tape," and a program never had to be redone.

We are often asked if our work puts stress on our relationship. Quite the opposite. We find that applying our skills to our own relationship makes it increasingly enjoyable. Yes, the sex is terrific, whether lying in bed with the sun beaming through the southern exposure bedroom window of our condominium, to times of excitement and sexual intimacy on a secluded beach on the Island of St. Lucia, or on grassy secluded areas of our parks in Canada. Perhaps helpful is the fact that between us we have 109 years of sexual experience.

Who are the Chernenkoffs? Both born and raised in Saskatchewan, we were married August 18, 1962, while Carolyn was in University, degree nursing, and William was in medical school.

After completing our degrees and raising 2 children, Tamara and Markel, we wanted to be in a career where we could work together as a team. In 1974, we studied with Masters and Johnson in St. Louis, Missouri and have been co-therapists in marital and sexual counselling since 1975. As well as our private practice, we are both part-time faculty at the College of Medicine, University of Saskatchewan, teaching sexuality to medical students and residents.

We are active in Continuing Medical Education Programs across Canada and appear frequently on various talk shows across Canada.

For five years we have had a regular *Relationships Column* on CBC Radio, *Afternoon Edition*. For eight years we have been regular guests on the STV television show, *Colleen & Company*. We have also been regular guests on the CBC television national program *What on Earth*.

For fun we like to play tennis, travel, relax on a beach and sleep.

Photograph by John Embury

William Chernenkoff, Colin Grewar, Carolyn Chernenkoff

WHAT YOU DON'T KNOW MAY HURT

COLIN GREWAR: Let's talk about sex. Uh huhhh, I caught your attention, didn't I? You know, we don't talk about sex very much, and for that reason many myths still exist about it. Marital and sexual co-therapists, Bill and Carolyn Chernenkoff, join me now to clear up a few of those myths. Hello, Bill and Carolyn.

CAROLYN: Hello, Colin.

BILL: Hi, good afternoon, Colin.

COLIN: I think it's important that we do this because, you know, when it comes to sex, what you don't know, may, in fact, hurt you.

BILL: It sure can. People can get into behavioral patterns that can be very destructive.

COLIN: We've got a list of sex myths, and we're going to speed through them. I've got the list in front of me, so I'll introduce the first one and then hand it over to you, Bill and Carolyn. The first myth that we're going to talk about is *Real men don't express their feelings.*

BILL: Yes. That's a common one. Maybe we can explain it by recounting a scenario that we saw in Waskesui this past summer. There was a family group, with some friends. A four-year-old boy in the group fell into the water. The water was cold. They fished him out of the water, and he was shaking, and upset. He was just on the verge of crying. His father patted him on the back and he said, "Tommy doesn't cry. He's a big boy." You notice what happened? He was being taught, right at age four, to suppress his feelings.

CAROLYN: Uh huhhh. Usually what happens, Colin, is that there are only certain feelings that are permissible for men to express. Usually they're aggression, competitiveness, anger and joviality.

(laughter)

BILL: Joviality, yes, he should be jovial.

CAROLYN: There are not many relationships that are based on those feelings.

BILL: Exactly.

CAROLYN: And just to give you an idea of what, very often, may happen is, the female may say to her partner, "What's the matter, what's wrong?"

BILL: "Nothing, nothing's wrong."

CAROLYN: "Well, something's the matter. How do you feel?"

BILL: "I'm fine, I'm just fine."

(laughter)

BILL: You notice what's happening? Here's Tommy, twenty, thirty years later. What's he learned? He's learned, "I don't share my feelings. I'm not vulnerable. If something is bothering me, or I'm upset about something, I hold my feelings in." And that's a passive aggression. Remember we said that we teach males to be aggressive, competitive, etc. By saying nothing, I'm controlling the whole situation.

COLIN: It's so important for parents to teach their young sons, right off the bat, that it's okay to cry.

CAROLYN: Yes, and daughters too.

BILL: Yes, to be tender, to be warm, to cry, to have feelings, to have emotions, and to be able to express them, that's wonderful. That's what builds intimacy.

CAROLYN: Yes, exactly.

COLIN: The second topic or myth – *Lovemaking will always be wildly exciting.*

CAROLYN: Yes. *(laughter)* Oh, we see this one a lot, Colin, and what happens is, when a relationship first begins, very often the lovemaking may be ecstatic, explosive, an avalanche of sensations. But after the couple are together for a while, it may just be pleasant or satisfying or comfortable, and that's perfectly fine as well. We liken it to this – if you're very hot and thirsty, and you have a glass of ice-cold water, it's tremendously refreshing. But if you're cool and you're not really thirsty, well, the glass of water is just a glass of water. So, it depends on what's gone on during the day, as to what the lovemaking may be like later on in the evening.

BILL: Sometimes it can be wildly exciting, but it can also be very enjoyable if it's just good.

CAROLYN: Right, sometimes the relationship mellows out.

(laughter)

COLIN: And it's always intimate, which is very important.

BILL: Exactly. You've got it, Colin.

COLIN: Number three – *Foreplay is just a prelude to real sex.*

BILL: Well, this is a really common bugbear; we hear it repeatedly. You know, studies have been done that say that the average couple, after they've been married for a while, take thirty seconds before they get to the breasts and genitals. That's how quickly loveplay or foreplay is dispensed with. You notice we're beginning to replace the word *foreplay* with the word *loveplay*. Because foreplay always gives the impression that something has to come after.

CAROLYN: And what we see happening, Colin, is if there is always the feeling that, when they begin, they have to end with intercourse, it puts a lot of pressure on either the male or the female. And so, very often, the female may not even express affection to her partner during the day. She may not hug him or cuddle with him, because she's afraid, if she does, this will indicate to him that she wants to have intercourse.

BILL: So, loveplay, or foreplay, may be the sex. *(laughter)* And, you know – many women would just love to be held, touched and caressed, without always having to have intercourse after.

COLIN: Just cuddling is okay.

CAROLYN: Wonderful.

COLIN: Topic number four, or myth number four – I should say, ***Sex should always be spur of the moment.***

CAROLYN: Yes.

(laughter)

COLIN: It gives you the feeling that if you plan it, it takes the fun out of it or something.

CAROLYN: Well, sort of – the feeling is that your day is so organized, and every hour is so accounted for that this is the last part of your life that may be spontaneous and romantic. But with today's society and the pressures that individuals are under, it's very seldom that sex can be just spontaneous. It's fine if it is, but what we have to look at – it's almost as if you have to plan things a little bit ahead. You have to make preparations. Suppose you're going on a picnic. Well, if you're going on a picnic, you have to plan ahead. You have to have gas in the car. You have to have food in the fridge, the freezer packs in the freezer. The same is true with romance. You may have to plan ahead. The children may go to visit the grandparents. You may have to arrange for supper or pick up supper on the way home, prepare the setting, so that the potential is there for feelings to surface.

BILL: What happens is, pockets of time are created by the couple. These pockets of time can be seductively planned, rather than waiting for an overwhelming feeling of desire that you can't control. Sometimes you have to plan ahead and not wait for the spur of the moment.

COLIN: Uh huhhh, because if you always wait for it to be spur of the moment, it might never be.

CAROLYN: How true.

(laughter)

BILL: And we see couples who wait for one year, two years. The perfect movement hasn't arrived and they have had no sex for that long.

CAROLYN: That's right.

COLIN: Myth number five – *If the sex was better the whole relationship would be better.*

BILL: Well, I have to agree that this is probably the most common male myth. We hear that repeatedly. I would say, Colin, we hear that once a week, at least.

COLIN: And generally from the male.

BILL: Exactly.

CAROLYN: Yes.

BILL: The male says, "You know, there's really nothing wrong with our relationship. If only we had better sex, more often, everything would be fine. There would really be no trouble."

CAROLYN: And usually, Colin, this is a male who is very distant, who is uncommunicative, who may be very controlling. He really has no relationship with his partner until the last thing at night when he falls into bed, and then he wants to have a sexual relationship. So, usually it is the female who says, "No, this is not right." If the relationship was better, then the whole sexual relationship would improve as well.

BILL: So actually, the truth of the myth, Colin, is the reverse way around.

CAROLYN: Yes. Good sex begins with your clothes on.

BILL: If the relationship is better, if there is more intimacy, then the sex does improve spontaneously. You know, it's interesting, and I guess it again stems from our first myth, very often males are task orientated. Sex is often seen as separate from the relationship. But when a male does realize that closeness and intimacy actually enhance the sexual relationship, that's when a better relationship improves his sexual enjoyment as well.

COLIN: Okay, onto our final myth for today – *Your partner will fulfill all of your sexual needs.* Now, Bill, Carolyn, surely you're not suggesting that we should seek sexual partners outside the marriage . . .

CAROLYN: . . . No . . .

COLIN: . . . Because that would be dangerous . . .

CAROLYN: . . . No, we mean within the committed relationship. But what we're looking at here is – often the female will say, "If my partner really loved me, he would know exactly what to do to turn me on, to meet all of my sexual needs; know what to do to arouse me." She puts the total responsibility on the male.

BILL: And you know, there are a lot of comparisons between sex and food . . . Because sex is a natural body function, the same as food and digestion. Suppose . . .

CAROLYN: . . . It would be the same as if the male decided when the female had an appetite for food, if he selected all of her food and told her what quantities of food she should eat and when she should sit down to eat, and then made sure she digested the food. If he did that, pretty soon she would be totally turned off to sitting down and eating with him. The same thing happens sexually. What we're suggesting here is that the female also has to take part. She has to be an active participant, and it should be something that the couple do with each other, rather than one person doing to or for the other person.

COLIN: Okay, Bill, Carolyn, we've discussed some of the most common sexual myths. I hope you've cleared some of them up for people.

CAROLYN: I hope so.

(laughter)

COLIN: Bill, Carolyn, thanks very much.

CAROLYN: Thanks, Colin.

BILL: Thank you, Colin.

QUOTES FROM COUPLES

I got my sex education from the V.D. films in the Army. Scared me to death.

I feel closer to a stranger sitting next to me on the bus.

We have a flawless marriage, we just don't have sex.

I've got him trained, why should I trade him off?

WHEN OLD FAITHFUL FALTERS

COLIN GREWAR: Hello, Bill, Carolyn.

CAROLYN: Hello, Colin

BILL: Hi, Colin.

COLIN: Now this session you have titled, "When Old Faithful Falters." . . . We're not talking about the family dog here . . .

CAROLYN: No. *(laughter)*

COLIN: . . . So, I'm going to let you lead us into this one. How about that?

BILL: . . . Actually, this is a very common problem. What led us to choose this topic is that we have frequently received letters from males, and sometimes females, telling us . . . that the sexual function of the male has diminished, and he's had difficulty with erections. They ask, "What should we do?"

CAROLYN: Although we title this one "When Old Faithful Falters," we're even seeing that young faithfuls may falter. It can happen to any age group. It's really very interesting, Colin. It's normal for any male to have problems with sexual response for up to a six-week period of time. That's normal and natural. For a male to think that he will never have difficulty with an erection would be the same as thinking he will never have a cold or he'll never have the flu.

BILL: And that's not realistic . . . right?

CAROLYN: It can happen any time, to any male.

BILL: Sure, but what happens is that when it does falter, the reaction that he has is very important.

CAROLYN: And his partner's reaction is also very important.

BILL: We have found that there's sort of . . . a recipe for psychological impotence that occurs.

COLIN: Okay, so we're going to talk about psychological reasons why a male might not be able to sustain an erection.

BILL: . . . Yes, and the psychological reasons are . . .

CAROLYN: . . . Well, the first one is . . . if the female leaves everything up to her male partner. He is supposed to know exactly what to do to turn her on. He is to orchestrate her sexual response. He's the person in charge.

BILL: So – she's passive; she really doesn't participate very much. She leaves it up to him, and he feels that he's the expert . . .

CAROLYN: . . . And she also expects him to be the expert.

BILL: That's right – and in order for her to be orgasmic, he's the one that gives her an orgasm, and he does it by intercourse alone.

CAROLYN: Uh huhhh.

BILL: Now, in order to accomplish all this – for this recipe to work – guess what has to happen? He has to have an erection to be able to do this. That's the most common pressure that males have. Sooner or later old faithful does falter and, of course, they're both devastated, because they have learned no other options.

CAROLYN: Now there are certain things that happens to the female . . . when the male begins having difficulty with his response. All sorts of things go through her mind. First of all, she wonders – "Am I less desirable to him." She also wonders – "Is he going outside our relationship – does he have a girlfriend . . . "

BILL: Or . . . "is he giving at the office?"

(laughter)

CAROLYN: Then, of course, what happens is that she may even confront him with that. She says, "Well, I know something's going on. You must have a girlfriend, You must be going outside our relationship, because you can't respond with me."

COLIN: Now the pressure's really on.

CAROLYN: Oh, is it ever.

BILL: Exactly. Not only has he lost his erection temporarily, but now he has this pressure from her . . . unless he can produce one, she's going to think he's interested in somebody else. That he's having a liaison with somebody else when, in reality, he's not.

CAROLYN: It may just be something like . . . stress for example. Losing an erection can happen very commonly when a person is under a lot of stress. For example, if he's a teacher . . . in June, when he's going through a lot of report cards . . . or a university student, when he's got exam week . . .

BILL: . . . Or a farmer in the springtime, and at harvest time. Those are very stressful times, and a lot of farmers are not too interested in sex during those times.

CAROLYN: Right.

BILL: You see, if he tries to force himself to have an erection, to try and please his partner, because she's not participating – she's playing a passive role – guess what happens? There is a tremendous amount of pressure which can develop into a fear of performance.

COLIN: And along with all the other stress that he's feeling at that particular time, I guess . . .

BILL: Exactly.

CAROLYN: The way he needs to handle it is . . . when the response is not there, if he says, "Okay, this is one time, I understand the stress that I'm under, it'll probably come back when the stress is removed – everything will probably work out okay." But if he says, "Oh, my gosh, this is heavy duty, this is the beginning of the end." Then he begins to develop a fear of performance.

BILL: And the fear of performance, of course, is that he watches to see if he's going to be able to have an erection to try and satisfy her, and to prove to himself that he's still a functioning male . . . rather than enjoying whatever happens. Then, when he misses and fails a couple of times, he avoids the situation. And then she thinks, "Well, he's avoiding me, he's not interested in me anymore."

CAROLYN: So it becomes a vicious circle resulting in a fear of failure and any avoidance of any sexual activity.

BILL: . . . In order to break that circle, they need to sit down together, and he needs to be able to tell her exactly what's happening to him. If we can look at a couple doing that – using some very effective skills and sharing their problems. We'll call them Sam and Jean. Sam says . . .

SAM: "You know, I'm going through a lot of stress."

JEAN: "Uh huhhh."

SAM: "I just want to let you know, I realize that our sex life has been less active lately. It's nothing that you're doing that isn't correct, or that I don't care for you anymore. It's just that I'm under so much stress right now, but I know it'll be over in a month's time, when this business crisis is finished. Then I can get back to spending more time with you."

JEAN: "That makes me feel better, because I felt it was something that I was doing that was wrong. I understand the amount of stress you're under, and I guess what's happening between us is normal. I would expect it under these circumstances. I would just like to be able to lay down and cuddle, without any expectations. I'd really enjoy that, just the closeness, just the intimacy."

SAM: "Oh really, and you mean, you touching me?"

JEAN: "Yes."

SAM: "Oh, that'd be nice."

JEAN: "Yes – so no goals, no expectations."

BILL: You see, Colin, she begins to take on a little more responsibility for the sexual interaction as well. That takes a tremendous amount of pressure off of him, and he verbalizes that. He shares what's happening, rather than holding it all in and pretending that he's waiting for some huge response.

COLIN: And I guess what might happen in the case of the woman in the relationship is that she will start feeling inadequate herself?

CAROLYN: Yes. She begins to wonder, "Have I lost him – is he no longer attracted to me sexually? Is he not interested in me?" And so, all the fears begin to creep in. Then she begins to wonder, "What am I doing wrong? Maybe it's my fault? What should I be doing differently?" So, if he explains exactly how he's feeling, it also alleviates a lot of her fears as well. If she doesn't know what's going on and she doesn't know what the problem is, automatically she thinks in the negative, and she thinks it's her fault.

COLIN: Now you mentioned that it's normal to have a loss of erections for a period of six weeks, Bill, Carolyn.

CAROLYN: Yes.

COLIN: But when and what are the signs when perhaps . . . it's a bit more of a problem?

BILL: Well, first of all, it is normal for males. If they lose an erection under stressful situations – Mother Nature still looks after things really well, what happens is that – in the mornings, when the male awakens, it is quite customary for him to have an erection. That means he's had an erotic dream or it may not even be associated with a dream – his bladder may be full, for example. That's a common occurrence. That's his little bit of insurance that, "Hey, things are working pretty well physiologically. I've just got to wait out the stress time, and it's all going to come back."

That's his sign that things are actually working okay, physically. Now, if after six weeks, he finds that there's no response with his partner; he's not waking up in the mornings with erections, then he may need to look at the possibility that there may actually be some physiological problems.

COLIN: I guess the overriding rule is – don't panic.

CAROLYN . . . Exactly, it's really interesting, Colin, we accept other things when we're under stress, that our appetites change, or we feel absolutely exhausted, but if any change occurs in the sexual response, we don't think that is normal, but it is.

BILL: Exactly we had one fellow who summed it all up for us. After the erections began to return, he said, "You know, I learned something interesting." We said, "What was that?" And he said, "Well, I found out that erections are like city buses . . . if you miss one, there'll always be another one coming around the corner."

(laughter)

BILL: That sums up exactly what happens. You don't have to panic.

COLIN: Okay, Bill, Carolyn, thank you very much.

CAROLYN: Thanks, Colin.

BILL: Our pleasure.

QUOTES FROM COUPLES

I used to touch his genitals at arm's length.

It was a half-hearted erection.

WHEN WOMEN LOSE THE DESIRE FOR SEX

COLIN GREWAR: It takes two to tango, as they say, and if one partner in a relationship has little interest in sex, it can lead to problems. A few weeks ago, marital and sexual co-therapists, Bill and Carolyn Chernenkoff, talked about the problems that occur when the male isn't exactly willing in the bedroom. Today we're going to discuss the causes of female loss of sexual desire. Hello, Carolyn, Bill.

CAROLYN: Hello, Colin.

BILL: Hi, Colin.

COLIN: What are some of the main reasons a female does lose interest in sex?

CAROLYN: The predominant one that we see, Colin, is when the female is in a relationship where there is a tremendous amount of control by a very domineering male partner. He corrects her all the time. He tells her how to live her life, just to try and make things a little bit easier and better for her.

BILL: And very often it's disguised as . . . the fact that he cares for her so much. This is really, by far, the most common cause.

CAROLYN: . . . And very often she'll say, "I feel I can't share any feelings, especially negative ones, with my partner. He feels he has to have a solution for them. He's always telling me what to do."

BILL: Maybe if we meet Tony and Grace . . .

CAROLYN: . . . And they can sort of illustrate what happens.

COLIN: Sure.

CAROLYN: Grace is working, and she's very successful in her job – she comes home and says . . .

GRACE: "I just had a really frustrating day. I had a tremendous workload, and I'm just exhausted. I'm really tired."

TONY: "Well, you know, Grace, if you would only do things differently, just the way I explained it to you. I think I've explained it to you a hundred times over and over. You really – you shouldn't back down at work. You have to be more assertive. You have to be more aggressive; they tend to walk all over you at work. I mean, you sort of back down and sometimes you act like a wimp."

GRACE: "You don't understand."
(laughter)

COLIN: He sounds like he's got all the answers.

CAROLYN: He has got all the answers!

COLIN: He thinks he does anyway, but how does that carry on into, you know, nothing happening in the bedroom?

BILL: Right, Colin, so far we've discussed nothing about sex, have we?

COLIN: That's right.

CAROLYN: He is continually controlling her, telling her how to live her life. It's not only her work, but it's all the subtle little innuendos and put-downs . . . He'll say things to her like, "Don't go out and get the milk. I'll get it for you, because you'll probably get the wrong kind." He makes her feel belittled. It lowers her self-esteem, so she feels that . . . while she is competent in other areas, at home she feels very unworthy and very incompetent. It takes away her desire and her interest in sexual activity as well.

BILL: As Tony was relating this, Grace was halfway out the door.

GRACE: "I was out the door."

(laughter)

GRACE: "I don't want to listen to this. Don't tell me. I can look after my own life."

CAROLYN: So it's a real turnoff.

BILL: And later on, as they're getting ready to go out socially . . .

CAROLYN: . . . They have to attend a social function. She has her makeup on. She's putting on her pantihose. They have fifteen minutes before they should be going out the door.

BILL: And Tony says . . .

TONY: "Wow, how about a little sex?"

GRACE: "Uh."

CAROLYN: She knows if she doesn't go ahead, he's going to pout, and he's going to be owly all evening, so she agrees.

BILL: He's Mr. Tony Testosterone. He's sort of ready to go any time.

CAROLYN: He thinks he's a tiger.

BILL: Yes! Tony the Tiger, and so every time he sees his partner in whatever state of undress, he's ready to go.

CAROLYN: And that's a real turnoff for her. Very often what she begins to do is agree just to please him. Sex becomes an obligation and duty.

BILL: And that's the key. As soon as she switches over to having sex just for him, rather than for herself, that suppresses her desire.

COLIN: Yes! Because when you're having sex under those circumstances, the actual act itself probably isn't a whole lot of fun. It's sort of a turnoff.

BILL: Exactly.

CAROLYN: Very often females say, "I'm getting nothing out of it, and the only reason I'm having sex is for my partner. I'm just agreeing when I feel I have to." There are other complicating factors too, Colin. Very often the female may have been brought up with the feeling that sex is bad, it's wrong, it's dirty, until you get married. And then when I ask these women, "What did your mother or your parents tell you what sex would be like after you were married?" They say, "They never told me about that part."

(laughter)

CAROLYN: So, sex is bad and sinful and dirty before you get married, and then there isn't any information that it's supposed to be different after marriage. The negative attitudes, combined with a very stressful relationship, don't allow her to develop more positive attitudes and feelings.

COLIN: I guess then, also, you can throw in the problems and pace of everyday life in the '90s . . .

BILL: . . . Yes, exactly, that's a common problem. We call them the lustbusters, work, family duties and children. There are also some physical causes that can inhibit sexual desire in the female. These are things that are gynecological problems, for example, pregnancy itself is not a gynecological problem, it's a natural state, but it does decrease desire in a lot of women.

CAROLYN: Yes, and then after delivery, there is a decrease in the estrogen level, the walls of the vagina may be thinner. There may be less lubrication, and sex may be uncomfortable for her, so she may delay having a sexual relationship after a pregnancy just because it hurts.

BILL: Now that's quite common, and it's important for couples to know that it's not going to stay that way indefinitely. When we're taking histories we ask, "When did the problem start?" And they very often relate, "After pregnancy number one or after pregnancy number two, that's when the problem started."

CAROLYN: Right. Usually the pregnancy is not the cause for the ongoing distress, but it may be the excuse! Some couples say, "Well, we don't have a sexual relationship because our three-year-old is sleeping with us every night." The couples that really want to have a relationship make sure the three-year-old is in his or her own bed.

COLIN: So there are a variety of reasons, but I guess the main reason extends from the relationship itself. Bill, Carolyn, how can you turn around the Tony and Grace type of situation?

BILL: Okay, well, why don't we have a look at Tony and Grace. Tony has now learned some skills to build up this relationship rather than destroy it. What Tony needs to do is so simple. Let's listen to Tony and Grace now . . .

GRACE: "Well, I've just had a really exhausting day, Tony, a tremendously heavy workload. It was very frustrating and I'm really tired. I'm just wiped out."

TONY: "Well, Grace, I can understand how you feel. I know you put a lot of effort into your work, and I really appreciate that."

GRACE: "Thank you, that makes me feel better. I just want to sit down, have a cup of tea and just relax for a little while."

TONY: "I'd like that, Grace, I'll get the tea and I'll join you."

GRACE: "Okay."

CAROLYN: He doesn't have to have a solution. All he has to do is accept what her feelings are and let her work it out.

BILL: And actually, for Tony, if he gets rid of this attitude of try-ing to make her a better person, by telling her what to do, it lifts a huge burden off his shoulders. And he's going to have a closer, more intimate partner, who wants to sit down with him instead of leaving the room.

(laughter)

CAROLYN: She feels more confident, and it builds up her self-esteem.

COLIN: Now, I bet a lot of couples wouldn't even realize that something like that is really at the root of – the cause of loss of female sexual desire.

CAROLYN: That's right, Colin, exactly. Usually it's the female who comes in. . . . She says, "This is my problem," and the male says, "It's her problem," but it's not. It's the interaction between the couple that is causing her distress.

BILL: Sometimes they say, "Just make the sex part better, and everything else in the relationship will be okay," and the reverse is true. Make the relationship better, and the sex part improves.

COLIN: Okay, Bill, Carolyn, thanks very much.

CAROLYN: Thanks, Colin.

BILL: Yes, thank you, Colin.

QUOTES FROM COUPLES

When I have sex with my husband, I can see my mother standing at the foot of the bed watching me.

Having sex with my husband is less desirable than brushing someone else's teeth.

ANORGASMIA, G-SPOT & FAKING IT

COLIN GREWAR: When it comes to sex, the orgasm seems to be the be all and end all, yet some women are anorgasmic. They don't reach orgasm when they have sex. Dr. Bill and Carolyn Chernenkoff are co-therapists in marital and sexual counselling in Saskatoon, and they join me now to share the truth about anorgasmia. Hello, Bill, Carolyn.

CAROLYN: Hello, Colin.

BILL: Hi, Colin.

COLIN: How common is this, for women to have sex without reaching an orgasm?

CAROLYN: Well, Colin, about ten percent of all women, at some point in their life, are anorgasmic. They don't reach an orgasm. For them, that is normal for that particular time.

COLIN: Huuum, what sort of an effect does it have on her?

CAROLYN: Well, it varies. Some people say, "I can still enjoy the relationship, and I have no problem. I really enjoy being close to my partner." Other people feel, "This is okay, but I would really like to be orgasmic." It varies a great deal from person to person.

BILL: You know, Colin, the person who should realize whether or not it is a problem for her, is the female, not the male, She is the only one who will know that. We have a situation with Rob and Nancy to illustrate this!

COLIN: Rob and Nancy, okay.

CAROLYN: Rob and Nancy are a young couple. They've just had some close, intimate relationship or experience, and this is what Rob says to Nancy . . .

ROB: "Did you reach it, Nancy?"

NANCY: "No, but it was really nice."

ROB: "Oh, not again. Look, I never had this problem with anybody else. I mean, what am I doing wrong?"

NANCY: "I don't know what you're doing wrong. It doesn't really make that much difference to me, but I really feel like I'm letting you down."

COLIN: They're both feeling kind of inadequate.

CAROLYN: Oh yes, Colin, and we have even seen females who have said, "It doesn't make that much difference to me, whether I'm orgasmic or not, but I'm even afraid to get into a relationship because of the pressure my partner puts on me."

BILL: Now, you see, Rob is sort of playing the teacher, the coaching role. He wants to get her to respond the way he thinks that she should respond.

CAROLYN: She says, "It doesn't make that much difference to me," but the key phrase here is, "I really feel I'm letting you down." There begins to be almost a search party for the orgasm. It's as if, women sometimes have a romantic idea that a knight in shining armor will come, and he will make everything happen for them. As one woman said to us, "Someday my prince will come, and I'll come too."

(laughter)

CAROLYN: There's the expectation that he will know everything.

COLIN: Yes, when we ask, the question, "Why is this happening," I guess it's partly because the female has to take more responsibility for the orgasm.

BILL: Exactly.

COLIN: I was wondering if it has anything to do with finding the sort of mystical G-spot that's . . .

CAROLYN: Oh yes, Colin. Actually, the G-spot, came out in the fifties. It was discovered by Dr. Graphenberg.

COLIN: Oh, that's why it's the G-spot.

CAROLYN: Yes. We actually have a whole cartoon book on the pursuit of the G-spot, which was not to be found. It was supposed to be a small area, about the size of a very small pea, on the front wall of the vagina. If you could find this G-spot, this tiny area, it was supposed to send women into ecstasy.

BILL: Wasn't that a wonderful fantasy, Colin.

COLIN: And you're telling me they've never found it.

BILL: There have been claims that people have found it and researched it, but it has not been proven.

CAROLYN: No.

BILL: In reality, there are lots of G-spots, all over the vagina and the entire body. Basically, closeness and intimacy are probably the biggest G-spot.

CAROLYN: What happened is, it put a lot of pressure on males to find it, and a lot of pressure on women to have it. It went out with the pet rock, but we still have questions about it.

COLIN: You know, given the pressures that we've discussed already, a male may put pressure on a female to have an orgasm, and a female puts pressure on herself to have one, all sorts of things. The female may be inclined to fake it. Is that a healthy thing to do, or not?

CAROLYN: Colin, remember the movie, "When Harry met Sally," and that restaurant scene where Harry said, "Well every woman

I've been with has always been orgasmic." And Sally said, "You wanna bet."

BILL: Harry thought that he was such a good lover that he would know if a woman was faking it.

CAROLYN: Yes, so she went through the sounds and motions of a complete orgasm. It was really graphic, and in front of the whole restaurant. It was just wonderful, probably a better orgasmic response than most women have ever experienced.

BILL: And if you kept your eyes closed, you would absolutely believe that this woman was having an orgasm. Nearby a woman was watching, and when the waitress came up to take an order from her, and said, "What would you like?" The woman said, "I'll have what she's having."

COLIN: Right, one of the more famous scenes in recent movie memory, that's for sure.

CAROLYN: Yes, exactly, but what it really shows is that it's sort of an easy way out. What happens then, is the female is trading approval for pleasure. She's searching for approval rather than telling her partner what's wrong, that she's not orgasmic . . . She's trying to build up his ego. She's trying to make him feel good, but what happens in this situation is that she doesn't get in touch with her own feelings.

BILL: Exactly.

CAROLYN: So, really, what a female needs to do if she finds that she's not reaching orgasm, has more to do with herself, giving herself permission. She has to be in touch with her emotions and feelings, and know what feels good for her. The male can't give the female an orgasm, like a gift-wrapped present.

BILL: A male won't know what turns a female on unless she knows.

CAROLYN: Yes. She is the authority on her own body. Fifty percent of women need more stimulation to reach orgasm than just the penis inside the vagina.

BILL: You see, the more that she learns about her body, about exploring, about the sensations that she can develop, the better the sex gets for her.

CAROLYN: That's right. Sometimes, Colin, we get too hung up on performance. I remember we had one man whose wife was not orgasmic, who said to us, "It's like putting a crop in and never seeing the harvest." We get too goal-orientated. Many women who are anorgasmic enjoy their partner, they enjoy life, they enjoy the pleasure in the sexual relationship without reaching an orgasm.

BILL: We had one woman recently tell us that . . .

CAROLYN: She said, "I've never reached an orgasm, so I really don't know what I'm missing, but I sure know when I'm having a good time."

(laughter)

COLIN: Okay, so sex can be gratifying even without the orgasm.

CAROLYN: . . . It depends how the female feels about it. If it's meeting her needs, she should enjoy whatever is happening. Orgasms are like dessert at the end of a meal. Sometimes you want dessert and sometimes you don't.

COLIN: Okay, Bill, Carolyn, thanks very much.

CAROLYN: Thanks, Colin.

BILL: A pleasure, Colin.

QUOTES FROM COUPLES

Female partner says, "I would like a dignified orgasm."

WHEN MEN FAKE ORGASM

COLIN GREWAR: Bill and Carolyn Chernenkoff are co-therapists in marital and sexual counselling in Saskatoon. A couple of weeks ago, they talked about anorgasmic women, women who don't have an orgasm when they have sex. Many of these women end up faking orgasm. Well, men fake orgasm too, and that's what Bill and Carolyn are going to talk about today. Hello, Bill, Carolyn.

CAROLYN: Hello, Colin.

BILL: Hi, Colin.

COLIN: Now, why would a male fake an orgasm?

BILL: Well . . . for too many people, intercourse or sex means having an orgasm at the end. What happens is that the expectation is there, and sometimes, just like anything else, the orgasm is not coming. Basically, to save face, the male fakes it. That's the purpose of it.

COLIN: He would be aroused in every other way?

BILL: Yes, he would.

CAROLYN: Yes, Colin. The arousal is fine, that all works, but if he's not going to reach an orgasm, he may fake it in order to draw the whole situation to a conclusion. It's a way of saying, "This is the end," rather than letting his partner down and making her feel that he just does not have any interest any longer. Sometimes, if he's not orgasmic, he's afraid that his partner may feel rejected.

BILL: Exactly.

COLIN: Now, are there specific causes for a man having trouble ejaculating?

BILL: Well, there are some definite causes, and we'll go through several of them. A simple one is sometimes when he's just had one too many beer.

CAROLYN: Yes.

BILL: . . . Now we're not saying one beer, we're saying one too many beer. Sometimes he comes home, and he is aroused, but he tries and tries, and he's just not able to reach an orgasm. So he just simply feels, "Well, this can go on indefinitely," and he does fake it.

CAROLYN: He feels that nothing is happening at all. It's his escape. Now, that may happen from time to time, and it's not really a problem. When he's not had too many beer, everything works perfectly fine. But there is a medical condition that actually is called ejaculatory failure. These are the ones that we see, the males that really have a sexual dysfunction.

BILL: One cause is when the male is really angry at his partner.

CAROLYN: Yes, at his female partner.

BILL: And it may be a legitimate anger.

CAROLYN: Yes. He may feel, "She has caused me so much pain that I may be in a sexual relationship with her, and I may have arousal, but I can't cross that threshold to orgasm." So it doesn't happen when he's with her.

BILL: Now another example may be that when he was younger, as a child, his older teenage sister may have become pregnant.

CAROLYN: It may have caused, Colin, great distress for the family. He was younger, he was growing up in the situation, and he remembers, vividly, his parents saying to him, "Don't you ever get a girl pregnant." Of course, he conditions himself then, so it never happens. He doesn't ejaculate into the vagina.

COLIN: That's all he's thinking about, is it?

BILL: He can't make the light switch turn on. When he gets married, he just simply is not able to ejaculate into the vagina.

CAROLYN: Yes.

BILL: That's not an unusual situation. Now, the last cause we see, and probably a more common one, is when a couple have been waiting. They decide to get married, and they're waiting for this best day of their life.

CAROLYN: Yes. The wedding day. Let's listen to Sarah and John. This is their wedding day, and they have just returned from the reception. They're in their hotel room.

BILL: And it's late.

CAROLYN: Very late.

BILL: . . . They're exhausted, and Sarah says to John . . .

SARAH: "It's been a wonderful day but exhausting. I'm absolutely wiped out. There are people coming early in the morning for the gift opening. I have to get some sleep. Do you think maybe we could do this in ten minutes maximum?"

JOHN: "I'll try."

CAROLYN: And he tries.

BILL: And he tries.

CAROLYN: They both realize that nothing is working and they are both absolutely devastated.

BILL: And he begins to condition himself so that the harder he tries, the less likely it is that he'll reach an orgasm. *It becomes emission impossible.*

(laughter)

COLIN: So, from that one incident, he goes into every other sexual approach . . . worried that he's not going to be able to ejaculate.

CAROLYN: That's right, Colin, and then there's almost a double pressure on him. When she finds out, she very often says to him, "Well, if nothing's happening, if you're not ejaculating, maybe you're not attracted to me, or maybe you don't love me. Why isn't it occurring with me?" So then he has a double pressure. First of all, he's trying so hard, and secondly, if he doesn't ejaculate he's letting her down.

BILL: Exactly. He puts himself into a pattern of faking it, because that way, at least her feelings are not hurt.

CAROLYN: Yes.

BILL: And he doesn't feel deflated either.

CAROLYN: No, which is quite interesting, because it is actually the mirror image of a female in the same situation. But, very often, people don't realize that it happens to the male too.

COLIN: Well, wouldn't it be kind of hard for a male to fake an orgasm?

BILL: Well, actually, no. It's much easier than we think. He will very often have all the sound effects . . .

CAROLYN: Yes.

BILL: . . . of what is appropriate.

CAROLYN: Yes, and the usage of tissues.

(laughter)

BILL: That's right. And if we keep in mind that the ejaculation contains approximately ½ to 1 teaspoon of semen . . . that's a very small quantity. There are normal secretions in the vagina itself, so it's very difficult, inside the vagina, to be able to tell whether ejaculation actually has occurred.

CAROLYN: Yes, he can go through the whole process and act it out, just the same way that a female may fake the situation too.

COLIN: They could both be faking it!

(laughter)

CAROLYN: Actually, we've never seen a couple where they both have, but that's mind boggling.

COLIN: So, when does the female find out and when does this become a problem that you might see?

BILL: Well, one time is when pregnancy does not occur.

CAROLYN: Yes.

BILL: . . . When there's no ejaculation taking place in the vagina, pregnancy is very difficult.

CAROLYN: Exactly, so we usually will see them because they want to have a pregnancy.

BILL: But sometimes the female just does find out. She suddenly discovers, just by something he says, that he has been faking it.

CAROLYN: And then, when it comes to light, very often they both decide that they want to have some help, because they don't want this to continue. Obviously, he doesn't want to live this situation over and over again. And they find out that it's really affecting other areas of the relationship.

COLIN: Yes, and I guess . . . once she's found out that he's been faking it, probably after that you can forget any chance of having an ejaculation.

BILL: That's right, it generally compounds the problem, because he's now really under pressure. He feels he's totally inadequate.

CAROLYN: They're both monitoring all the time.

BILL: But there is good news. This is a very reversible problem.

CAROLYN: Yes, and the way to reverse it is to look at "What is the cause?" When you can look at the cause, then you can begin to remove those roadblocks. Then everything will happen spontaneously.

BILL: Remember, we said earlier that, for too many people, good sex equals orgasm at the end?

CAROLYN: But in reality, good sex means whatever is enjoyable and satisfying to both individuals, rather than having the orgasm tacked on at the end as the objective. When you take away the pressure, the orgasm surfaces naturally.

COLIN: You've cured the problem.

CAROLYN: Yes!

COLIN: Okay, Bill, Carolyn, thanks very much.

CAROLYN: Good, thanks Colin.

BILL: A pleasure.

QUOTES FROM COUPLES

I am not orgasmic. I wish to be otherwise.
So does my husband.

I felt I was pouring out love through the skin.

Premature Ejaculation

COLIN GREWAR: As is the case every other Tuesday, I'm joined now by Dr. Bill and Carolyn Chernenkoff. Bill and Carolyn are co-therapists in marital and sexual counselling in Saskatoon, and today we're going to discuss the most common male sexual problem – premature ejaculation. Hello, Bill, Carolyn.

BILL: Good Afternoon, Colin.

CAROLYN: Hello, Colin.

COLIN: Well, the first thing we have to establish here is how fast is too fast. When does eager become premature ejaculation?

(laughter)

BILL: Oh, that's beautiful. I like that. Well, a definition we tend to use is that if the ejaculation occurs sooner than what is necessary for the female to have high enough levels of arousal to have enjoyment or to be orgasmic.

CAROLYN: Right, but usually the couple knows, Colin. They know, this is just too soon . . . we don't put a time limit on it. We usually leave it up to the couple, as to what they feel is too soon.

BILL: And while it is a male dysfunction . . .

CAROLYN: . . . It's a female distress.

(laughter)

CAROLYN: It causes more distress to the female because she's left frustrated each and every time. So, usually, it's the female who initiates seeking help or treatment.

COLIN: So, how does it affect them in their lives together?

BILL: Well, what happens is that sex gets increasingly frustrating for the female.

CAROLYN: Yes, she feels he's so selfish.

(laughter)

CAROLYN: She thinks he's doing this intentionally, and if he really wanted to, he would be able to delay the ejaculation. He's getting satisfaction out of it, and she's getting nothing out of it. What happens is that she gets resentful, angry and frustrated. The anger just seethes out of her. She gets very annoyed at him.

BILL: We brought along Cindy and Ron . . .

COLIN: . . . Cindy and Ron?

BILL: . . . They typify, in a brief scenario, what happens when there's premature ejaculation.

CAROLYN: So, Cindy says . . .

CINDY: "Ron, if you really wanted to, you could do something about this. This is your problem. I feel frustrated, and I feel used each time this happens."

RON: "I'm sorry, Cindy . . . I'll try harder next time."

CINDY: "There may not be a next time!"

BILL AND CAROLYN: Ooooh! (simultaneously)

(laughter)

COLIN: I guess one of the long-term effects is that they probably just don't have sex as much as . . .

BILL: . . . Exactly.

CAROLYN: What happens, if this has been occurring for a period of time, the female may develop inhibited sexual desire. That may be how they present it to us. She says, "I don't want to have sex with him any more." But when we take the history, very often the cause is because the ejaculation is occurring so soon.

BILL: What you pinpointed is what happens. She tends to touch him less and less. She thinks he'll get aroused too quickly.

CAROLYN: Right, she stops touching him. There's no holding of any kind, no caressing. She's not getting aroused. They just go ahead and have intercourse, and it's all over so quickly.

COLIN: Do we know what causes premature ejaculation?

CAROLYN: Actually, we do.

BILL: It's not a physical medical problem, it's a conditioning pattern. It's basically always caused by two things. The first is based on the first one or two experiences that the male has. They may happen to be rapid, hurried situations where he's afraid of being discovered. He may be in the back seat of a car or in his parent's house and he feels that he's got to have it over with as quickly as possible. That sets the pattern for him and, interestingly enough, there's nothing he can do to change it.

CAROLYN: Right.

BILL: Not every male who has that experience will become a premature ejaculator, but every male who has premature ejaculation will have a history like that in his past.

CAROLYN: That's one cause, and the second cause is that the male may not have had a problem until later on in the marriage. When his partner really doesn't enjoy sex, and she says, "I'll go ahead for you, but just get it over with as fast as possible." So he conditions himself to be very quick and that pattern can lead to the premature ejaculation. But there's no specific physical cause for it occurring, and there's no medical prescription that can change it either.

COLIN: So, how do we solve the problem?

BILL: Well, first of all . . . Cindy and Ron try all kinds of things . . .

CAROLYN: . . . The home remedies . . .

BILL: We've heard just about everything, one of the home remedies is putting ice cubes on the testicles . . . ooooh!

(laughter)

CAROLYN: Very uncomfortable . . . Counting backwards is another one.

BILL: Or sometimes a male tells us, "I mentally take my car or my watch apart."

COLIN: Try to think of something else – unhappy thoughts.

CAROLYN: That's right, Colin. As he's doing that, though, he's distracting himself, and as he distracts himself, he also loses his level of arousal. That's another interference factor as well, loss of arousal leads to loss of erection. So, none of these work.

BILL: Another one that is commonly advertised in magazines, that we would like to discuss, is the cream to slow down arousal. It is an anaesthetic cream. And so, it may anaesthetize the penis somewhat, but . . .

CAROLYN: It also anaesthetizes the vagina as well, so both individuals, the male and female, just have this numbness, no feeling at all. So that doesn't work either.

BILL: It's not a good home remedy.

CAROLYN: No.

BILL: But there is a good treatment for it.

CAROLYN: . . . What we do, Colin, first of all we need to see the couple, and we need to look at their communication skills, and also neutralize the anger and frustration that the female has.

COLIN: Obviously what Cindy and Ron were doing wasn't right.

CAROLYN: Exactly. It's also necessary to educate both of them – for her to know that he's not doing this willfully. He's not able to control it once the pattern has been established. But there is a technique that the two of them can learn together. It's not something that the male can do himself. It is a technique that the female can utilize, and in that way she can delay the ejaculation. It's called the "squeeze technique" and we actually teach the female, using the "squeeze technique" on her thumb. Then when they're in the privacy of their own home, she doesn't use it on her thumb . . .

(laughter)

COLIN: Uh huhhh. I get the picture.

CAROLYN: . . . It's unique and specific for each individual couple, but it's very, very effective. It's just amazing when I teach these women how to use the "squeeze technique" on the penis. I've never seen people take on new instructions with the enthusiasm that these women do, because they say, "Finally, there's something I can do. I have some control over the situation."

BILL: And that's an important key. She's not doing this for him, she's doing this for herself. And, the irony about it is that as she participates more to delay the ejaculation, for herself, not for him, she begins to touch more, to become more involved. There's less hesitation about touching . . . and what happens is that more arousal surfaces in her. She basically turns herself on by touching her partner.

CAROLYN: Right, and then as she's using the squeeze technique, she's also able to delay the ejaculation, so they have a much higher level of enjoyment for a longer period of time. It all works very effectively. So, if you're going to have a dysfunction – a sexual dysfunction, this is the one to have.

(laughter)

BILL: The best one.

CAROLYN: . . . Because the success rate of the "squeeze technique" is about ninety-five percent.

COLIN: Oh really.

BILL: Yes. It really works.

COLIN: But I guess the key is . . . it's funny, but . . . the female is actually the one that has to almost solve the problem here.

BILL: The male cannot do this for himself. It has to be done with the female.

CAROLYN: Right, so it may be a male dysfunction, but he needs to have a willing female partner in order to reverse the distress.

BILL: It's very effective, and it's delightful that the couple learn so easily. They utilize the "squeeze technique" for approximately a six-month period of time. After that they gradually use it less and less, but they always have the skill. If the problem ever surfaces again, they can retrain the penis again . . . it really works.

COLIN: Okay, Bill, Carolyn, thanks very much.

CAROLYN: Our pleasure, Colin.

BILL: Thank you, Colin.

QUOTES FROM COUPLES

He starts. He finishes.

He had an immature ejaculation.

Why Is Our Sex Life The Pits?

COLIN GREWAR: Why is our sex life the pits? That question echoes through many bedrooms. In fact, fifty percent of all couples have some sort of distress or sexual dysfunction at some time in their relationship. While sexual response is a natural body function, there are roadblocks that can interfere with that response. Joining me now to talk about those roadblocks are Dr. Bill and Carolyn Chernenkoff, co-therapists in marital and sexual counselling in Saskatoon. Hello, Carolyn, Bill.

BILL: Hi, Colin.

CAROLYN: Hello, Colin.

COLIN: We're going to work through about four or five of the most common barriers that you find on the road to a happy sex life. The first one, Bill, is **fear of performance.**

BILL: Fear of performance, that's a common one. This is where the person begins to be afraid that he or she is not going to perform or function the way they, or their partner, expects them to. Colin, let's have a look at a couple as the therapist is taking a history from the male. We'll call them Mr. & Mrs. Fail.

CAROLYN: So, I'm going to be the therapist, Colin. I say to Mr. Fail . . .

THERAPIST: "Mr. Fail, when you approach your partner, what's the first thing that goes through your mind?"

MR. FAIL: "Well, what happens is, I worry that the machinery just is not going to work, I mean, the darn thing just won't stand up. I get so worried that my hands get all cold and clammy and moist, so when I touch my partner, that's what I feel, moisture and clamminess, so I just sort of leave it up to her. I don't approach her any more."

THERAPIST: "Yes, Mr. Fail, I understand."

CAROLYN: Here Mr. Fail is expressing the fear of performance. He's afraid it's not going to work, and then what happens is, automatically, it doesn't work. His concern and fear prevent the "machinery" from working. He uses these terms almost as if it's not part of his body that doesn't work but part of a machine.

BILL: Exactly, as if his erection is going to be turned on like a button . . . that's the fear of performance. You notice, Colin, he actually led into the second barrier. What did he say? He said, "So I don't approach her any more." That's the **fear of failure**.

COLIN: Fear of failure?

BILL: Right.

CAROLYN: And the fear of failure is this . . . the person feels it didn't work last time, it's not going to work this time, and it's probably not going to work in the future either, so why should I even try. After a period of time he convinces himself that he's going to fail, so he avoids the sexual interaction. He stops approaching his partner; he leaves it up to his partner to approach him. He is thoroughly convinced it's not going to work.

BILL: And sometimes we hear people saying, "I'm so busy with everything else. My job is keeping me away." Very often they create an environment for themselves which takes them away from having the opportunity to approach their partners, because it's so scary for them. Therefore, they avoid the situation.

CAROLYN: Or else they make sure their partners go to bed first and are asleep for maybe half an hour before they even go into the bedroom. They're afraid that if they're in bed, their partners will approach them sexually.

COLIN: In the meantime, the other partner's in bed wondering, "Why is my sex life the pits?"

BILL: Exactly, they're not even together.

(laughter)

COLIN: Let's move on to the third roadblock. You described it, Bill and Carolyn, as the **spectator role**.

BILL: Yes.

CAROLYN: The spectator role is this, Colin. Mentally the person is sitting up in a corner, watching to see, "How am I doing?" So they're monitoring all the time, "What's happening, what's going on?" That's one part of the spectator role. There's another part as well, and maybe we can just role play that.

BILL: Let's briefly have a look at Mrs. Fail's history. The therapist is asking Mrs. Fail . . .

THERAPIST: "Mrs. Fail, when you're with your partner, and he's touching you, what's going through your mind?"

MRS. FAIL: "Well, my body is there, but my mind is elsewhere. I'm thinking of almost everything else I possibly can. I'm going over my grocery list. I'm thinking of everything that I have scheduled for the next day. My mind is clicking all the time. So, physically, I'm there, but my mind is in a different place, and then I think, why should I even bother getting involved in this because it's not going to work anyway, and I'm just going to be left frustrated."

COLIN: Hummm.

BILL: See what's happened. She's dissociated herself – she's somewhere else mentally and not involved.

CAROLYN: Women very commonly do this. They're thinking about almost everything else, more important matters, maybe the grocery list, things that they have scheduled for the next day, almost everything but their sensations and pleasure. They need to be able to bring these two parts together, the body and the mind.

COLIN: Do you think, Carolyn, women are more guilty of this . . . or more susceptible to this roadblock?

BILL: Well, it can actually be either male or female. Let's put it this way, I think that males experience the spectator role just as frequently. But males are more often watching to see whether they're performing correctly or not, whereas, women tend to think of their grocery list a little bit more often.

CAROLYN: Because there isn't as much pressure on females, visually, to appear to be responding or performing.

BILL: . . . Exactly. They don't have an erection to lose.

CAROLYN: . . . So the female can think of other things and her partner is not aware.

BILL: Whereas with the male, if he's thinking of his car or grocery list, guess what happens? "The machinery ain't workin'."

(laughter)

COLIN: Everybody knows . . .

BILL: Exactly.

COLIN: A fourth roadblock you described as the **double standard**.

CAROLYN: Oh yes, yes. This is one we see commonly. . . .

BILL: . . . And the double standard is, I guess initially, it's called the "good girl syndrome."

CAROLYN: . . . We've never really been able to define a "good girl" but most people know what it is. Females grow up not knowing anything about their own body or about sexuality. But when they get married, they're going to be with a male that will know everything. Because we all know that when boy babies are born, they know everything about sex, just like that . . . automatically.

(laughter)

CAROLYN: And so those females feel that their male partners will know everything, not only about the male's own sexual function but about the female's as well.

BILL: Ironically, the male usually does grow up thinking that **he is** the authority. When he realizes that he does not know what to do to turn her on . . . he keeps doubling his efforts to do so, but, of course, that puts her into a terrific bind.

CAROLYN: Right. She feels that she has a passive role, and she leaves everything up to him. He is the one that is going to orchestrate her sexual response. He's in charge.

BILL: Exactly.

COLIN: And he feels that he should be.

(laughter)

BILL: Yes.

CAROLYN: Yes, and if he doesn't, he really feels . . .

BILL: . . . That he's failed, and that, again, leads to the fear of failure that we talked about earlier. There is also another aspect of the double standard.

CAROLYN: Right. It develops later on in the marriage, and it works this way. The good girl very often develops "the good wife syndrome," meaning that whenever the male feels that he wants to have sex, she should be there for him, whether she wants to or not. She should go ahead out of a sense of obligation and duty, and you can imagine how much of a turn on that is for her . . .

COLIN: Yes.

CAROLYN: That doesn't work.

BILL: And guess what happens to her if she keeps on having sex with him as an obligation and duty? It becomes another job and she just gets frustrated about the whole situation.

CAROLYN: Then she just throws up her hands and says, "I don't want to do this anymore. I don't want to have a sexual relationship with you anymore." It's total frustration.

BILL: And he says, "Forget it."

COLIN: Having sex out of a sense of obligation just doesn't give much motivation, I guess. The fifth roadblock and I guess this may be the key to it all, Carolyn and Bill, is **breakdown of communication.**

CAROLYN: Yes.

BILL: Absolutely. It's either a breakdown in communication or even a nondevelopment of communication. A lot of couples say, "Gee, you know, we communicate really well. We talk a lot." But basically what they talk about, if we really look at it, is about parenting roles, about finances, about their jobs, or whatever, but they really don't get down to the feelings that they have about themselves, about their partners. This results in intimacy and closeness not being there, that's what's missing. When we say, communication breakdown or nondevelopment, it's the intimate close communication that's lacking.

CAROLYN: Or else they talk about other things, but because the sexual relationship has not been working well, they're afraid to talk about it. It's really taboo. And we say that communication is the blood supply to the relationship. It brings in the nutrients and it takes out the garbage.

BILL: It's absolutely essential.

COLIN: How, Bill and Carolyn, could improved communication help in a situation, for example, where there's a fear of failure? Where they think, it didn't work last time, so it's not going to work this time.

BILL: Good question, Colin . . . Actually, what you've asked just now is part of the therapy. We have the person verbalize just that every time they are afraid of failure. Mr. Fail, in the privacy of his bedroom, is asked to share his feelings verbally with his wife.

MR. FAIL: "I'm really afraid. I feel scared that this is not going to work, and I feel clammy and cold."

MRS. FAIL: "I understand how you feel."

BILL: What happens is, as soon as Mr. Fail identifies his fear, and his partner accepts it, and communicates that maybe she has her own fears, ironically, that's what gets rid of the roadblock.

COLIN: Okay, Carolyn, Bill, thanks very much.

CAROLYN: Thanks, Colin.

BILL: Thank you, Colin.

QUOTES FROM COUPLES

Female partner talking about male partner -
"We can't get an erection."

He gets an erection when he knows I'm menstruating.

I have no problem reaching an orgasm
as long as my husband is not in the room.

DEALING WITH CHILDHOOD SEXUAL TRAUMA AS AN ADULT

COLIN GREWAR: The trauma and distress experienced by a child who is the victim of sexual abuse does not disappear as that child grows older. As adults, these victims often have difficulties in marriage or in developing intimacy. Joining me now to talk about coping with childhood abuse as an adult, are Dr. Bill and Carolyn Chernenkoff, co-therapists in marital and sexual counselling in Saskatoon. Hello, Bill, Carolyn.

CAROLYN: Hello, Colin.

BILL: Good afternoon, Colin.

COLIN: Very serious situations evolve from childhood abuse . . .

CAROLYN: Yes. This is a heavy one.

BILL: Yes.

COLIN: . . . This sort of thing, do you see a lot of it?

CAROLYN: We do, Colin. We take histories from every couple that we see and in taking a history we always ask, "Were you frightened sexually, as a child, or did you go through some sexual trauma?"

BILL: And, of course, statistically, as we know, one of every four females and one of every ten males, has had some sort of sexual trauma, It's a very common thing.

CAROLYN: And what happens, Colin, is that even though this trauma occurs, it doesn't necessarily have a lifelong harmful effect. What we mean is that, sometimes when a couple comes in, and the male presents us with a sexual dysfunction, in just taking the history from the female, we find out that she may be a survivor of sexual trauma. Sometimes she has worked through it, has had counselling, and it really isn't affecting her in the relationship. It has been dealt with very well. In other instances it can have a profound effect. When we do ask the question, "Were you a victim of sexual trauma," and she says, "Yes," if she has not dealt with it, it may have led to her developing any of the sexual dysfunctions that we see in females.

BILL: Exactly.

COLIN: What are some of the things that you see, in a person, or in a relationship, when one person has suffered abuse as a child.

CAROLYN: Well, certainly we see inhibited sexual desire.

BILL: If it's been the female who has had the sexual trauma, inhibited sexual desire is probably one of the most common symptoms.

CAROLYN: Yes, and then, of course, the other symptoms we see are anorgasmia, in females, also vaginismus, which is involuntary muscular contraction of the first one third of the vagina, and lastly, we see sexual aversion in the female. In this case, whenever she thinks of sexual activity, or if her partner approaches her, she has a reaction of almost phobic proportions or she experiences flashbacks.

BILL: Now, Colin, males have a slightly different symptom pathology. They can develop premature ejaculation. They can develop erectile dysfunction. They can have ejaculatory failure or inhibited sexual desire. Now, although sexual abuse is less common in males . . . it's equally traumatic for the male. We don't anticipate, in our society, that a male, who's supposedly macho and in control . . . will be abused. And so it's sometimes even more difficult for him to deal with it. Now, we should clarify, Colin, as Carolyn said initially, sometimes we take the history of a couple, and there is really no distress or dysfunction in the female related to childhood sexual trauma. That's a credit to the Sexual Abuse or Sexual

Assault Centers that we have in Saskatchewan and other provinces. They give excellent counselling. Sometimes such care is not available for the male.

CAROLYN: Yes, we do find, Colin, that people have gone through excellent healing processes, with the help of the Sexual Assault Centers. These people don't need our counselling. They have dealt with the trauma.

BILL: Exactly.

CAROLYN: So, that counselling really is a benefit and a help. But those who do have distress, whatever dysfunction they may have, there are certain things that commonly show up. Maybe we could role play what could happen when we're seeing a couple. Suppose it is the female who is the survivor of the sexual trauma.

BILL: She's the one who's been affected by this, and now it's affecting her in the relationship, in the intimacy, just as you noted in your opening remarks. If we could just have a glimpse of a very brief segment of her history. Would that be okay, Colin?

COLIN: Sure.

BILL: We'll call them Mr. & Mrs. Jones. Mrs. Jones is having her history taken . . .

THERAPIST: "Mrs. Jones, when your partner approaches you intimately, sexually, what do you feel?"

MRS. JONES: "I feel absolutely nothing. I feel like I'm numb, I have no feelings at all. I just feel dead."

THERAPIST: "What do you think should happen?"

MRS. JONES: "I would like to feel some arousal, because I really love my partner. I really care for him, and I would like to feel something happening. I'd like to know that I'm normal. I'd like to know that everything functions."

THERAPIST: "And so when you do touch, or he touches you, what happens?"

MRS. JONES: "I feel nothing."

BILL: Do you see what has happened, Colin?

COLIN: Hummm.

BILL: She has dissociated her feelings from her body . . .

CAROLYN: . . . In order to cope . . . and first of all, she needs to be given credit in that whatever she had to do, she did right at the time in order to survive. So whatever way she coped was the right way for her. But she can learn again to get in touch with her feelings. We'll just take a look at dissociation. We all dissociate. We get into a car, and we get from point A to point B, and we know we arrive where we're supposed to get to, that we're there, but we don't know how we maneuvered, looked at the cars, drove through the lights and everything. That's dissociating, and that's normal. But when a person is put in a traumatic situation, very often they separate their feelings from their body, and that's what she's done . . . just to survive the traumatic situation.

BILL: So, let's have a look at how Mrs. Jones, now in therapy, can get in tune with her feelings, rather than dissociating them and putting them aside.

CAROLYN: In the beginning, we have her look at being able to bring her feelings to the fore, without having anything sexual attached to those feelings since, at this stage, it would be too frightening.

BILL: Exactly. So, we're going to look at a very brief segment of something that goes on much more extensively.

THERAPIST: "Mrs. Jones, you're sitting at the table . . ."

MRS. JONES: "Uh huh."

THERAPIST: ". . . And your hands are on the table. Put your fingertips on the table, and touch the table gently with your fingertips. Just describe to me, what do you feel?"

MRS. JONES: "Well, there is a tingling sensation. The table sort of feels leathery, it's warm and it has a fine grain, that's what it feels like."

THERAPIST: "Now, Mrs. Jones, if you take your fingers and just put them on your jacket, on your sleeve, how would you describe that texture?"

MRS. JONES: "It's a thicker texture. It feels warm, a little bit warmer and smooth."

THERAPIST: "Uh huhhh! Now if you'll just take your hand and put your fingers on the other hand, just imagine that is your partner's hand and arm. What textures do you feel?"

MRS. JONES: "I can feel veins, and I can feel the hair and the skin, and it's warmer. I can feel the bones underneath and the ligaments in the hand. I can feel that."

THERAPIST: "Mrs. Jones, that's terrific. That's exactly what I need to have you do when you're with your partner. Just focus in on what those feelings and sensations are."

MRS. JONES: "Okay, I can do that."

CAROLYN: So, instead of her looking for arousal, what we have her do is begin to touch her partner for her own experience, and find out just what the sensations are.

COLIN: I guess, Bill and Carolyn, that the treatment has to involve both partners in a relationship . . .

CAROLYN: Yes.

COLIN: . . . And I'm wondering what the other partner . . . is supposed to do in this situation.

BILL: You're absolutely right.

CAROLYN: Yes, that's a very good question, Colin.

BILL: You see, already we notice that Mrs. Jones is beginning to have some feeling of warmth emanating. She is describing sort of a nonsexual warmth.

CAROLYN: She has feelings she is beginning to identify just by touch. That's what she wants to know. She wants to know that she is a person who has feelings.

BILL: Now, Mr. Jones also has a very important role. Very often Mrs. Jones' partner says, "Well, it's her problem," but it's not.

CAROLYN: Mr. Jones often thinks that maybe she can just get help by herself, but she can't. It's an interaction in which she needs a very supportive, caring partner.

BILL: Suppose Mrs. Jones is now learning to tune in to what her feelings are, but if her husband doesn't know how to handle that situation he, unknowingly, may actually suppress her progress.

CAROLYN: Yes.

BILL: For example, if we have a look at Mr. & Mrs. Jones in the privacy of their bedroom and we hear a dialogue like this . . . .

MRS. JONES: "When you approach me, I feel a tremendous amount of fear. I have flashbacks, and I get very frightened and very panicky."

MR. JONES: "Well, you know, that happened a long time ago. You really shouldn't feel that way. I mean, we're married now, we've been married for years. You really don't have to feel that way. For heaven's sake, why do you do that?"

MRS. JONES: "OK, I'll try not to . . . ."

BILL: Now, you see what happens.

CAROLYN: Yes, you see what happens, Colin. She has . . .

COLIN: He's not very sensitive. He is not accepting her feelings is he?

BILL: No.

CAROLYN: . . . She has opened up and got in touch with her feelings. She's validated those feelings, which is very important for her, and he has negated them – with good intent. He's trying to make her feel better. He says, "You shouldn't feel that way. I care for you. I love you. Try and get rid of them." But of course, that pushes all those feelings back inside.

BILL: Exactly. Unknowingly . . .

CAROLYN: . . . Yes . . .

BILL: . . . Thinking that if he can only convince her not to have those feelings, that she'll feel better, but in actuality, that's putting a cap on them right there.

COLIN: How should he react?

CAROLYN: We'll go through it again . . . So if Mrs. Jones says . . .

MRS. JONES: "When you approach me, I just feel very afraid. I feel almost a panic reaction. I have flashbacks, and I'm very frightened."

MR. JONES: "Well, I can understand that. Sometimes I don't understand, I guess, but deep down I really think I can understand. I care for you, and I just want you to know that any time you want me to stop, that's okay with me. I just enjoy being with you."

MRS. JONES: "Okay, that's what I needed to hear. That makes me feel better."

CAROLYN: Okay, Colin, see what's happened?

BILL: What's happened is that she has control over her feelings, which is crucial, and she is getting those feelings out rather than suppressing them.

CAROLYN: And she also feels that he has accepted her feelings, that it was okay for her to have those feelings. So she feels also that at any time she can stop or she can slow down, and she has control over what she's doing, not control over him but control over herself.

BILL: And so, by accepting her feelings, he may not understand them, because he may not have had the experience, but he can accept that that's okay. Those are valid feelings. Those are normal things to happen under the circumstance, but he still cares for her and he can accept her. They can stop and do other things or come back to intimacy at a later time.

CAROLYN: So the other part of the equation is that, whoever is the survivor of the sexual trauma, whether it be the male or the female, that person needs to be always in control of themselves during the sexual relationship, so they're never put in the position of doing something they don't want to do . . . When both partners in the relationship have counselling . . . excellent results can occur.

COLIN: Okay. Bill, Carolyn, thank you very much.

CAROLYN: Good, thanks, Colin.

BILL: Thanks, Colin.

QUOTES FROM COUPLES

Show me an equal partner and I'll show you better sex.

When we told our six-year-old that we were going to have counselling, he said, "It's about time."

MOST COMMON CAUSE OF UNCONSUMMATED MARRIAGES

COLIN GREWAR: Despite what you may think about the sexually liberated times in which we live, many couples enter into marriage without ever having had intercourse. In some cases, even months after the wedding day, the marriage remains unconsummated. We're going to discuss that today on our relationships column. Dr. Bill and Carolyn Chernenkoff are co-therapists in marital and sexual counselling in Saskatoon. Hi, Bill, Carolyn.

CAROLYN: Hi, Colin.

BILL: Good afternoon, Colin.

COLIN: . . . An unconsummated marriage – it's got kind of a legal ring to it. How exactly is it defined?

CAROLYN: Unconsummated, Colin, is defined this way – if ejaculation has never occurred inside the vagina, that means the marriage is unconsummated.

BILL: That's actually the legal aspect of it, and the most common reason for it to occur, is a medical problem, called vaginismus, where intercourse is virtually impossible. That's the most common reason.

COLIN: So, what is vaginismus?

CAROLYN: . . . Vaginismus is an involuntary muscular contraction of the first one-third of the vagina. What actually happens is the muscles surrounding the outer one-third of the vagina go into spasm, so the couple are not able to have intercourse. Also, the female is not able to have a pelvic examination by a physician. She's not even able to have a pap smear, it's not possible to insert anything into the vagina. (See the photograph on page 65.)

COLIN: What are the causes of vaginismus?

BILL: Well . . . there are a number of causes. One common cause is a girl growing up in a parental background where, unintentionally, her parents may exaggerate things in a negative way. For example, the child may hear – while her mother is having coffee with friends around the kitchen table, "Oh, do you know what I went through when I had my daughter? It was **so** painful." Sometimes parents will even use this as a threat. They will say, "You didn't get your homework done, why are you doing this to me. Do you know what I went through when I had you as a baby? All the pain I went through?"

CAROLYN: Sometimes mothers exaggerate the delivery stories, about how long and uncomfortable the labor and delivery was. What happens is – the female is afraid of being hurt in the vagina. Also, another common cause is when a girl is brought up with very negative attitudes about sexuality and doesn't know anything about her own body. She doesn't know anything about sex in general or her own body specifically. She is taught very negative attitudes about sex before marriage, and then is not able to turn the light switch from sex being bad, before marriage, into sex being wonderful and positive after she gets married.

BILL: Another cause is gynecological problems, for example, infections may cause discomfort. There are also a variety of medical problems that can occur. Even though the medical cause may be treated successfully and long gone, the pattern of the protective response to prevent pain which results in involuntary, muscular contractions, continues on.

COLIN: So it's very often psychological . . .

BILL: . . . Right, we must stress though, Colin, that these are perfectly normal, healthy women. In fact, virtually always, these are very intelligent females, and very often they are very successful in their work.

COLIN: So, what can vaginismus do to a relationship?

CAROLYN: Well, it's very interesting, Colin . . . These are often really committed relationships. With vaginismus, we have seen couples who have been married for a couple of months, the most common situations that we're seeing now are couples that have been married for two or three years. But we have seen two couples that have been married for nine years, where they tried every week to have intercourse and were unsuccessful. And the surprising thing is – of all the couples that we have seen, not one of the males has gone outside the relationship. They're very committed to each other.

BILL: Yes.

CAROLYN: . . . What happens is this . . . the female leaves everything up to the male. Usually she's very dependent on him, even though she's very intelligent. He generally looks after her. She has a normal interest and desire for sexual activity, and she has a normal response, but she's just not able to have intercourse. So they have other forms of sexual response not dependent on intercourse. Very often they will seek help, first of all, because they want to have intercourse, and secondly, because they want to have a pregnancy.

BILL: And that's fascinating, because they just accept . . . that they're not going to have intercourse. But, of course, it's difficult to get pregnant . . . and that's very often why they seek help.

COLIN: Well, what you say is interesting, these people you see are committed people in committed marriages. But I would imagine that there are lots that you don't see, and this condition causes the breakup of many relationships.

BILL: Oh yes, and I think that's very observant, Colin. There are probably couples who have just simply never realized that help is available, and they just end their relationship as an unconsummated marriage.

CAROLYN: Yes.

BILL: But the key is – your observation is very important – the majority of people don't realize that there are a lot of other people out there with exactly the same problem.

CAROLYN: I guess, too, Colin, they expect that when they get married, and they try to have intercourse the first night of the honeymoon, that everything will work spontaneously and naturally. When it doesn't, often they are absolutely devastated. They feel that they are the only people in the world that this has happened to. In talking to the female and getting a history from her, she will say, "I think I'm different from anybody else. I'm so unusual." She will very often even feel that she's made differently. She will say, "I'm sure there's a bone there. There's something preventing intercourse from occurring," when, of course, there isn't a bone there. It's just that the muscular contraction is so strong that they're not able to have intercourse.

COLIN: And there is treatment available. What does it consist of?

BILL: – The success rate for this type of problem is very, very high, a ninety-eight percent success rate. There are two things – number one, the relationship needs some therapy, because the female partner needs to take on more responsibility for her own sexual function and experience. The male has to back off on some of the responsibility he has taken on. The second thing is that we teach the couple to retrain the muscles surrounding the vagina. The female basically retrains her muscles by using graduated dilators, so that she starts with a small dilator, which is comfortable for her, and then she gradually progresses to larger dilators, so that the muscles can actually be retrained so that they no longer go into spasm.

CAROLYN: Yes. Actually, she's able to do this quite quickly. She can progress through the different sizes of dilators almost daily, and she's able to learn how to be able to relax her muscles. She needs to feel that she's in complete control of the situation. Then she makes a transition from using the dilators to using the penis.

BILL: And Voila! They are having intercourse.

CAROLYN: Yes, the other part of it is that we very often need to look at the negative attitudes about sexuality that she may have been brought up with. She needs to change those attitudes to much more positive feelings about herself, about her body and about the sexual part of the relationship.

COLIN: I guess what I hear, just in closing, Bill and Carolyn, is that this is a common problem and it is treatable.

CAROLYN: It's very common.

BILL: . . . And people should feel free and confident about contacting their physician, because most physicians now are trained and well versed in being able to identify these problems. Help is definitely available.

CAROLYN: And the other thing, too, Colin, is that we find, as these women are able to retrain the muscles of the vagina, they develop a tremendous amount of self-confidence and self-esteem. We had one lady who also developed a tremendous sense of humor as well. She said when she went home she was going to take the dilator and put it on a gold chain around her neck, with the inscription, "In case of vaginismus, please insert."

(laughter)

BILL: It was just delightful to see the change.

CAROLYN: A very interesting couple.

COLIN: Bill, Carolyn, thank you very much.

CAROLYN: Thanks, Colin.

BILL: A pleasure.

Physician's glasses being crushed during pelvic exam.

QUOTES FROM COUPLES

I'd like to get pregnant if I didn't have to have sex to do it.

*I have not experienced orgasm during intercourse or
in any way associated with my husband.*

*A male phoned in on a Thursday wanting desperately to make
an appointment for Friday because he was getting married
on Saturday in Las Vegas.*

WHEN SEX HURTS

COLIN GREWAR: Sex is supposed to be enjoyable. It's certainly not supposed to hurt, and if it does, there is something wrong. Dr. Bill and Carolyn Chernenkoff are co-therapists in marital and sexual counselling in Saskatoon, and they join me now to talk about, "When Sex Hurts." Hello, Bill, Carolyn.

CAROLYN: Hi.

BILL: Hi, Colin.

COLIN: I guess the real difficulty here is that sex is something that people traditionally don't talk about too freely, and so, in many cases, someone won't even know that what they're experiencing may be wrong, or normal or not. Even when it hurts, they may think that's the way it's supposed to feel.

CAROLYN: Exactly, Colin. It may hurt even from the very beginning, and they've had no other experience, so they have nothing to compare it to. It's very important, if it is uncomfortable, to stop having sex and see a physician.

BILL: Exactly . . . have the problem looked into, because it should not be hurting on a continuous basis. Now, any one of us has backaches or leg aches that may occur. These are twinges that can be uncomfortable, but these are fleeting, and the same thing can happen with regard to intercourse, but if it's something that's going on and on . . . then definitely, that should be looked after.

COLIN: Because if it does go on and on, it can sure turn a person off.

CAROLYN: That's exactly what happens, Colin. It may begin with a physical reason, but if it continues for a long period of time, there begins to be a psychological component. Then they develop inhibited sexual desire, and they don't want to have sex at all.

COLIN: Now, you have provided me with a list of some of the more common reasons why sex may hurt. Let's just start and see how many we can get through here.

CAROLYN: Okay.

COLIN: The first one – **inadequate lubrication in the female.**

CAROLYN: Yes. Well, that's actually the most common problem that we see, and it happens for various reasons. It may be less estrogen, where a female is going through menopause. It may happen after the delivery of a baby, or if she is not getting aroused. She may be really angry at her partner and, in all of these, if there's no arousal, then there's no lubrication.

BILL: It sounds like it should just affect the female, but actually, at the risk of being facetious, it creates friction in the marriage.

CAROLYN: Yes.

(laughter)

BILL: Meaning that it can be very uncomfortable for the male as well, if there isn't adequate lubrication in the vagina.

CAROLYN: Right, it may even be caused by medications she is on. If, for example, she's on antihistamines, for a cold or allergies, that will also dry the vagina as well.

COLIN: So, are there cures for a dry vagina or lack of arousal?

BILL: Yes.

CAROLYN: There are. We actually have an easy solution.

BILL: One of our household hints.

CAROLYN: Yes, we have a household hint. We tell all couples we're seeing for counselling that – lubrication in the female is exactly the same as erection in the male, so if the female is not lubricated, the couple should not be having intercourse.

BILL: Exactly. We also give a little household hint, that it should always be the female who inserts the penis in the vagina.

CAROLYN: Right, always.

BILL: Always.

CAROLYN: And the reason is that the female knows if she's lubricated and if she's ready.

BILL: So we're going to rent billboards in North Regina and South Saskatoon that say, "it should always be the female who inserts the penis in the vagina."

CAROLYN: But we'll sign it "anonymous."

(laughter)

COLIN: Let's move on to another "When Sex Hurts" problem. How about **vaginitis**?

BILL: Vaginitis means an infection or inflammation of the vagina. It could be like tonsillitis or infection or inflammation of any structure. The most common cause is a bacteria or yeast infection. Usually there's a vaginal discharge, and there's discomfort with it. That's very easily treated. The female should see her physician. There's excellent medication available.

CAROLYN: Right, and we do say that if there's an infection, they should stop having intercourse until it's treated.

BILL: Right.

CAROLYN: Because if the cells are infected and inflamed, and if she continues to have intercourse, it's like having a scab on your finger and continually rubbing the scab off. It never heals. So she needs to allow those cells time to heal.

BILL: Exactly.

COLIN: Next on the list is **Peyronie's disease**.

BILL: Well, this is a male problem, and can occur in any age group, but certainly in the twenty to forty age group it is common. This is where a fibrous plaque occurs on the penis.

COLIN: What does that mean, Bill?

BILL: Well, what happens is that it's like a scar. It is a hard, thick elongated plaque, and it tends to curve the penis. The penis can suddenly begin to look to the right, or it can begin to look to the left or, most commonly, it sort of looks towards "the heavens." As a consequence, it's hard to angulate, or direct the penis into the vagina. It can cause a lot of distress and discomfort for couples, but good treatment is actually available now.

CAROLYN: The reason we brought that up, Colin, is, we recently got a letter from a couple. They said nobody ever talked about this problem, but it was something that they were dealing with, and they wanted some information about it.

BILL: First of all, a lot of the fibrous plaques do clear up on their own. Secondly, some of them need to be removed, through a very minor surgical procedure, by a urologist, or injected with Cortisone. It is very treatable. Couples don't have to suffer through it.

COLIN: Let's move on to another one, Bill and Carolyn. We talked about this before, so we'll just touch on it here, **vaginismus**.

CAROLYN: Vaginismus, this, Colin, is where the muscles surrounding the first one third of the vagina, contract right down. So the female says, "I feel like I'm built differently from everybody else. I feel there's a bone there." So every time she tries to have anything inserted in the vagina, she gets discomfort or pain.

BILL: I suppose it's like trying to park your car in the garage when the garage door is closed. It just doesn't fit. Basically that's a medical problem, and the therapy success rate for that is excellent.

COLIN: Moving on to another one – **the uncircumcised male** can have some problems.

BILL: Right. And, first of all, because the male is not circumcised doesn't mean that there'll be a problem. A lot of males are not circumcised, and that's a trend nowadays, but sometimes the foreskin can adhere to the head of the penis. There can be infection, there can be inflammation, or as the foreskin attempts to pull back, it can crack, and that can be very uncomfortable. There is medication available for that – it is very easily treatable.

COLIN: How about this one, **endometriosis** in the female?

CAROLYN: Endometriosis, Colin, is where there's tissue from the lining of the uterus that begins to grow in other areas inside the body. What happens, is that the female gets uncomfortable when she's having intercourse. That can definitely be treated medically as well.

COLIN: And one last physical problem that we have time to discuss here, Bill and Carolyn, is an **imperforate hymen**.

CAROLYN: The imperforate hymen, yes, and sometimes, Colin, that gets confused with vaginismus. What happens is the first time, as the couple begins to have intercourse, maybe the first night of the honeymoon, they find they're not able to. What actually happens is that the membrane of the hymen is very tough, and they're not able to penetrate it.

BILL: Virtually every year we see a couple with this problem. They started having intercourse after they were married, and it was very uncomfortable. What happens is, the hymen is being stretched inward, and it's almost forming a cup inside the vagina. So, basically, what they're ending up having is intercourse with the stretched hymen rather than with the vagina.

CAROLYN: Yes, it's very uncomfortable. So, remember, if it hurts, stop having sex. Talk it over with your partner and seek help right away.

COLIN: Yes, you know, Bill and Carolyn, I guess it's always hard for people in any circumstance to go to the doctor, and I would imagine that it's even harder when we're talking about our sexual parts, the most private parts of our body. What would you say to listeners out there who might have heard something that applies to them. The symptoms are something that they're familiar with, but they are just too embarrassed to seek help.

BILL: Sure, it is probably one of the most difficult things for people to talk about, but physicians now are really well trained and help is available. It's amazing how easy it is once they seek help.

CAROLYN: Right. You also need to say exactly when you're having the pain, and how it feels. If you just go in and have a physical examination, and don't explain that you're having discomfort, and expect the physician to pick it up, it is really not fair. You have to say exactly where the pain is.

BILL: I would definitely agree with that.

(laughter)

COLIN: Bill, Carolyn, thanks very much.

CAROLYN: Good, thanks, Colin.

BILL: Thanks very much, Colin.

QUOTES FROM COUPLES

My husband is so rough,
I'm sure I have callouses on my clitoris.

He is like a rabbit.

SEX AS AN OBLIGATION

COLIN GREWAR: Sex is supposed to be enjoyable, and it can be, so long as both parties are into it. If, say, the male feels he always has to go ahead and have sex when he doesn't feel like it, then sex becomes an obligation, and that's not good for either party. Joining me now to talk about this are Dr. Bill and Carolyn Chernenkoff, co-therapists in marital and sexual counselling in Saskatoon. Hello, Carolyn, Bill.

CAROLYN: Hello, Colin.

BILL: Good afternoon, Colin.

COLIN: I guess it's understandable that this would happen a fair bit, because no two people are alike. No two people share the same sex drive. You can't expect them to be totally harmonized sexually.

CAROLYN: Yes, that's exactly right, Colin. We get into relationships, and we see that we respect the other person as having differences, but we think sexually they should be our mirror image. They should have exactly the same desires.

BILL: It reminds us of the movie, *Annie Hall*, by Woody Allen.

CAROLYN: Yes, I think this movie was back in the '70s . . .

COLIN: Woody Allen and Dianne Keaton.

BILL: Yes, that's right.

CAROLYN: Colin . . . there is a scene in that movie, where each individual is visiting a psychiatrist. The psychiatrists are asking them separately, and what we as viewers see is a split screen . . .

BILL: So, both of them are on the screen at the same time.

CAROLYN: And each is being asked individually, in separate offices, by a psychiatrist, "How often are you making love?"

BILL: And Woody Allen says, "Well, practically never, I'd say three times a week."

CAROLYN: And Dianne Keaton says, "Constantly, I think three times a week."

BILL: So you see how the perception of an identical number by two people can be quite different.

CAROLYN: Yes, and what happens then is that one person may have a greater desire and interest for sexual activity, whereas the other person, who may have the lesser desire, begins to feel that they should have sex out of a sense of obligation.

COLIN: That takes all the fun out of it . . . Do you find that it's usually the male that has more desire and the female less, or does it work that way at all.

CAROLYN: It works both ways, Colin. In either the female putting pressure on the male, or the male putting pressure on the female.

BILL: Now we have Jim and Alice to illustrate how the male puts pressure on the female.

COLIN: Jim and Alice, okay.

BILL: Jim comes home from work, and as he enters, we hear this conversation . . .

JIM: "Alice, I'm home."

ALICE: "You're home early, Jim. It's about an hour before you usually get home."

JIM: "I got off earlier, and I wanted to . . . I know you like nice things done for you, so I got the drycleaning on the way home and I got you some flowers."

ALICE: "That's very nice, Jim, what's the occasion?"

JIM: "Well, today is Tuesday."

ALICE: "Yes, it's Tuesday all day. Yesterday was Monday."

JIM: "Yes Alice, well, Tuesday we have sex."

ALICE: "You've got to be kidding. I've got to carpool the kids, I've got to drive them to hockey practice; I've got to stay at the rink. I'm not going to be home until about 11:00 o'clock."

JIM: "Listen Alice, a guy needs sex!"

ALICE: "Well, maybe I'll get home fifteen minutes earlier and I hope you're in a better mood tomorrow."

JIM: "Well, I guess."

COLIN: Humm.

(laughter)

COLIN: He was all set to go, flowers and all . . .

CAROLYN: And these women say, "I go ahead because I don't want to put up with the anger or the pouting or the coolness. They get very resentful and very angry.

COLIN: Is there a similar sort of dynamic when it's the female putting pressure on the male?

CAROLYN: Yes, in fact, it's almost worse, Colin, in this way. Very often, the female, when she has a higher desire and a greater interest, doesn't approach her partner when she has that higher desire. She expects him to do the approaching, know when she wants sex, even though he's not as interested as she is, his desire is not as high as hers.

BILL: . . . He's got a double "whammy" of responsibility. First he should know when she is interested.

CAROLYN: . . . And also she feels it's his job to approach her, to arouse her, to satisfy and to meet all of her sexual needs.

BILL: In fact, if she would approach him, there might be less tendency for this problem to develop.

CAROLYN: So we have another couple . . .

BILL: . . . Janice and Larry.

CAROLYN: . . . Here are Janice and Larry. Janice is the pressure cooker in this situation, and she's putting the pressure on him.

(laughter)

CAROLYN: It's evening, and she says to Larry . . .

JANICE: "How come you're never interested in sex any more? You never approach me."

LARRY: "What do you mean, Janice? I sure do . . . but wait . . . there's something really good on *Newsworld* I wanted to watch, something's happening that's really important."

JANICE: "You're gonna stay down here and watch television again? I think you purposely wait until I go to sleep before you come to bed."

LARRY: "Do we have any beer?"

(laughter)

COLIN: Let's change the subject again.

BILL: Exactly.

CAROLYN: Yes . . . And what happens then is the person who has the lesser desire begins to avoid the potential sexual situation. The woman was busy in the carpool. This fellow's going to watch *Newsworld* until he knows she's asleep . . . He waits until she goes to bed, because he knows that then he can avoid his partner . . .

COLIN: Yes . . . They can avoid the situation. And how does it affect the person with the greater desire? Does he or she feel, I don't know, rejected or something?

BILL: Actually, what you bring up is very important. What happens is that the person with the greater desire level seems to double his effort. Here he will go through almost anything, like getting the drycleaning, getting some flowers. "I'll do anything for you, just so you'll be interested." But, it's another pressure added on to existing pressure.

CAROLYN: And then the guilt trip of the year is, "If you really loved me, you'd want to have sex with me!"

BILL: Yes.

(laughter)

CAROLYN: And of course, that makes the other person feel tremendously guilty. She feels . . . "I have to go ahead out of a sense of obligation."

BILL: Because the implied statement is, "You really don't love me, because you don't want to have sex with me," which is totally untrue . . .

CAROLYN: . . . It is untrue, because the number of times that you want to have sex is not a condition of how much you care for this person. It's just natural that you may have a difference in desire.

BILL: Exactly.

COLIN: And I guess, when they do have sex, it's probably not the greatest in the world, right?

BILL: Well, whenever a person goes ahead as an obligation, as a duty, he or she is really doing it as a chore. One more job at the end of the day.

CAROLYN: Yes.

BILL: Instead of getting involved in it and enjoying the multiple sensations that can happen, she's thinking, "I hope this is going to satisfy my partner."

CAROLYN: And the other person picks up on it. He knows very well the partner is only going ahead for him, so it also takes away his enjoyment as well. So, both of them, even though they may have had a sexual relationship, may feel very empty afterwards. There's not the intimacy or closeness there should be.

COLIN: So, as we stated when we started talking, it's understandable that this should happen, because no two people are alike. So how do we . . . ?

CAROLYN: . . . How do you change this . . . ?

BILL: A couple like this, actually, are both functioning very normally sexually. What's happened is just that the pressure has taken away the desire.

CAROLYN: Right. What they have to look at is, it's normal for individuals to have differences and different desires. What they have to do is sit down and assess, "Where are we at? How many times would each of us like to have sex." These differences may not be that great . . . it's just that one person is putting so much pressure on the other.

BILL: Because, just like Woody Allen and Dianne Keaton . . . they're really having the same number of sexual experiences, it's just the interpretation . . . So the person who is putting the pressure on needs to back off.

CAROLYN: And then they also need to look at, "What other factors may there be in the relationship that are taking away the desire?" Maybe there's a lot of stress going on outside the relationship or inside the relationship, besides sex. They need to look at those factors that can be changed. Also they need to look at – intercourse isn't the end all and be all. What did they do before they started having intercourse? Holding . . . touching . . . caressing? Are there other things that can be enjoyable for them, without it depending on intercourse.

BILL: So instead of this obligation of intercourse hanging over the person whose desire level may be slightly less, they begin to re-explore all the different things that they really enjoyed before they started having intercourse . . .

CAROLYN: Right.

BILL: It's amazing how that can reawaken the sensations and recharge a low-voltage sexual relationship very quickly.

CAROLYN: Also, if a person approaches another individual and the individual says, "No, not right now," and it's accepted by the initiator, it's much more likely that the person approached will want to go ahead the next time. When they feel pressured into it, that is the thief of desire. It takes away the interest.

COLIN: The thief of desire. If you do the right things, you can stop the thief of desire.

BILL: Absolutely.

CAROLYN: Exactly.

COLIN: Carolyn, Bill, thanks very much.

CAROLYN: Thanks, Colin.

BILL: Thank you, Colin.

QUOTES FROM COUPLES

Our problems are sex and money.
He doesn't get enough sex and I don't get enough money.

I solved the problem of my wife not wanting sex –
we have sex every Monday and then she doesn't have to worry
about it the rest of the week.

When my wife puts the KY jelly on the bedside table,
I know she's ready for sex.

Is SEX TAKING A BACK SEAT TO STRESS?

COLIN GREWAR: I feel totally stressed out. How many times have you heard that lately, or said it yourself? Stress is the condition of the '90s. It's affecting people at work, at home and in the bedroom. Joining me now to talk about sex and stress are Bill & Carolyn Chernenkoff, co-therapists in marital and sexual counselling in Saskatoon. Hi, Bill, Carolyn.

CAROLYN: Hello, Colin.

BILL: Good Afternoon, Colin.

COLIN: So, is sex taking a back seat to stress in the '90s?

BILL: Yes.

CAROLYN: Yes, it definitely is. Sex is sort of replaced right now by stress. Stress is the big S word of the '90s.

(laughter)

COLIN: Oh dear.

BILL: And sex and stress really are not good bed partners.

CAROLYN: No.

COLIN: It's sort of ironic, because it seems to me that we're seeing so much more about sex now on T.V.; we're talking about it much more freely now. It's everywhere.

BILL: We joke about it. We sell cars, tires and chocolates with it.

CAROLYN: Right. But we do find that more and more people are experiencing sex less and less. Very often it's because of the lifestyle and because they're suffering from chronic stress.

BILL: They're in the fast lane, but the only problem is that the fast lane takes them right past the sex part.

(laughter)

COLIN: So, what's changed in the '90s? People have always had to deal with stress. When you think back to the days when the settlers were founding this land, they didn't have a very easy time, so what's changed now?

BILL: Well, the economic conditions are changing. Job security is changing, people are facing bankruptcies. Actually, Colin, some stress can be good for you. It gets you motivated; it gets you to prepare projects you need to do; it gets you to study for exams. But if you're under constant stress all the time, with the uncertainty of knowing what your future is going to hold, that's where it can affect the sexual desire in both males and females.

COLIN: I guess here in Saskatchewan, with the downturn in the agricultural industry, you're probably seeing a lot of it.

CAROLYN: Yes, we do, Colin. That was why we picked this topic. It seems that we are getting more questions from couples. We seem to be seeing couples not so much with a sexual dysfunction, but they are in sexual distress. They're not able to function sexually. They have less desire, and then when they get into the bedroom, they find things just don't work.

BILL: So, sexually and emotionally, they are just simply in chronic constant distress.

CAROLYN: Yes.

BILL: Now, sexual dysfunction is normal when we're under stress. It's usually short-lived. Stress can affect many bodily functions.

For example, we may have a headache or an upset stomach. A lot of people can identify with that, they say, "Well it's because I'm under a lot of stress." But what a lot of people don't identify is that they may have a sexual dysfunction or shutdown occurring, and that's because of the chronic stress.

COLIN: I'm trying to distinguish here whether this lack of sexual desire is an emotional or a physical sort of symptom of stress? What would you say?

CAROLYN: It's emotional. And, of course, when people have less desire they may force themselves to say, "Can I make this work." When they do that, they find out that, for the female, she has less arousal, less lubrication. She may suddenly not even be orgasmic, when she was previously. It's as if, "Well I'm under all this stress, and now I can't even function sexually. This is the last straw. The last thing that I really need is a sexual problem."

BILL: And while it's emotional, actual physical symptoms can surface because of the chronic stress. People actually do get physical symptoms occurring.

COLIN: Yes, and as Carolyn was saying, if they actually do get around to doing it, getting the time and feeling the inclination and it's not working well, it's . . .

BILL: It's jinxed.

CAROLYN: Exactly. As one couple said to us, "It's sort of the icing on the cake of my day."

(laughter)

CAROLYN: So you think, "Well, I've got all this stress and now this on top of it all." But it's important to realize that when the stress is relieved, or reduced, the sexual function will come back spontaneously. The dysfunction is only temporary. It's important to not be concerned, knowing that, when the stress is relieved, everything is going to work.

COLIN: Does the stress affect males and females differently?

BILL: Actually, it does, Colin, because there's a different way in which males tend to handle it, as compared to females. The male very often becomes withdrawn, sometimes irritable and uncommunicative.

CAROLYN: The strong, silent type . . .

BILL: Yes, the strong, silent type. Actually, in a way, he's doing that to try to protect his partner.

CAROLYN: Right. But as he does that, she feels isolated and distanced from him. She very often feels rejected. Actually, we have a role play for this, Colin.

BILL: We have Cheryl and Kent with us.

COLIN: Cheryl and Kent?

CAROLYN: Yes. This is a young couple who are 35 years old . . .

BILL: . . . There are job insecurities occurring. We'll listen to what's happening.

CAROLYN: Cheryl says to Kent . . .

CHERYL: "What's the matter with you? I just don't feel you're communicating. I just don't know what's going on here. You don't say anything to me, what's the matter?"

KENT: "Nothing's wrong. Everything . . . everything is just fine."

CHERYL: "Well there must be something that's wrong."

KENT: "No, everything is fine, don't worry. Everything is just fine."

COLIN: Ummm.

CAROLYN: That's it.

COLIN: The strong, silent type?

CAROLYN: Yes.

BILL: You can just feel the distance between the two of them.

CAROLYN: This continues on until they get into bed, and then they're hanging on to their opposite sides of the bed. They feel very isolated and very much alone.

BILL: They may try to force their sexual response to occur under that circumstance and, of course, it just doesn't work.

CAROLYN: Right.

COLIN: So, what's the solution here, Bill and Carolyn, other than, oh, I don't know, quitting our high pressure jobs and retiring to a cottage somewhere in the remotest part of Northern Saskatchewan?

BILL: Oh, that sounds wonderful.

COLIN: That's not a bad idea, actually.

CAROLYN: Yes.

BILL: But that's not realistic.

COLIN: No, not realistic, unfortunately. What can a couple like Cheryl and Kent do?

BILL: Well, first of all, it's for them to realize that it is normal under conditions of stress for the sexual desire to wane for a while. We call it decreased libido or "lost lust." It occurs for a temporary period of time.

CAROLYN: Yes. And it's also important for him to be able to express his feelings and for her to be able to share her concerns. Then maybe they can handle it a bit differently. If Cheryl and Kent are able to share their emotions about this, she may approach it in a different way.

BILL: We hear Cheryl saying. . .

CHERYL: "I don't know what's going on, but I feel a tremendous amount of stress here."

KENT: "Well, I'm hearing about cutbacks, and I just don't know how secure my job is any more. You know Cheryl, I'm really worried."

CHERYL: "Well, that I can understand. Yes, I feel better knowing what the problem is."

KENT: "And you know, Cheryl, I never dreamt that I would be saying something like this and especially at my age, but, I don't even have the urge that often any more."

CHERYL: "Really. That I can understand too. And, you know, actually, I feel better knowing that because I thought it was me."

COLIN: Ah! A lot more communication. . .

BILL: Yes, the situation hasn't changed, they still have the job stress and insecurity, but even that is now a bond because they're sharing it, and working through it together.

CAROLYN: Yes. We invariably hear women say, "If my partner shares his vulnerability with me, I feel much better. I feel closer to him." And so it builds the intimacy in the relationship. They still may have the stress, but at least they're facing it together. They're a team, and she doesn't feel so isolated from him.

COLIN: And if things start working a little bit better on the communications level, it could be that the sex will improve.

CAROLYN: That's right, Colin.

BILL: You've got it. Because what happens is that instead of sex being a job, related to what's happening throughout the rest of the week, they approach it as a playful thing. When they leave the stress outside the bedroom, it's amazing, Mother Nature looks after the response instinctively. It'll surface and, actually, sex is a good stress reliever.

CAROLYN: Yes, it'll do the trick. It'll relieve the stress in absolutely the most ultimate form of communication. The couple will feel much closer together.

COLIN: Bill, Carolyn, thanks very much.

CAROLYN: Good, thanks, Colin.

BILL: A pleasure.

QUOTES FROM COUPLES

She may as well wear black panties – her orgasms are dead.

I'd rather work than share feelings.

A female partner to her male partner –
"Don't start anything you can't finish."

QUESTIONS OF COLLEGE STUDENTS

COLIN GREWAR: Dr. Bill and Carolyn Chernenkoff are co-therapists in marital and sexual counselling in Saskatoon. In the course of their work, they have given lectures at many colleges. Their talks always inspire lots of questions from the students. Bill and Carolyn join me now to discuss some of the things college students ask about sex. Hello, Carolyn, Bill.

BILL: Hi, Colin.

CAROLYN: Hi, Colin.

COLIN: You know, I'm trying to get a picture of this in my mind. I see you in front of a large crowd of students, and . . . how do they ask questions, do they stick up their hands and talk . . . because some of these questions could be sort of private.

BILL: Well, actually, from time to time they do just that. For example, we may have a group of five hundred students, and all of a sudden, a person will just put up his or her hand, and ask a question, but the majority are written down.

CAROLYN: What we do, Colin, is before we begin the talk, we pass pieces of paper through the audience, and we let them know that as we're giving the talk, we'd be very pleased if they would write down any questions. Then the questions are passed down to the front. At the interval between the first and the second sessions, we answer the questions.

COLIN: Now, over all, are you surprised at what college students know or don't know about sex.

BILL: They know a lot.

CAROLYN: Yes . . . and this is not just basic information. This is more about relationships, and it includes the whole spectrum.

BILL: Yes it's just fascinating. They're very open with questions. They're not afraid to ask questions at all.

CAROLYN: And some have never had sex, while others are very experienced sexually. Some are mature students; they may be married and may have many children. So we get questions from all levels.

COLIN: Generally, does it break down fairly evenly between men and women, do you find, or do you ever notice that?

BILL: I think, in general, it's pretty well half and half.

CAROLYN: I think so too.

COLIN: Well, you've provided me, Bill and Carolyn, with a list of some of the more common questions you are asked. Why don't I play the student here, and you can play yourselves.

CAROLYN: Okay.

BILL: Terrific.

COLIN: Okay, here's the first one. "Can you describe the difference in the type of orgasms which a woman has, and if I have orgasms when I dream, while asleep, why doesn't it happen in a waking state with my partner?" I hope her partner wasn't in the crowd.

(laughter)

CAROLYN: Usually they're there with their partners.

CAROLYN: Well, just to explain this, there may be many reasons or ways that the female may be stimulated but, actually, the orgasmic response is a total body response. It's not just a pelvic event, so there may be response with breast stimulation, there may be genital stimulation, there may be intercourse. We have even seen women recently who, without even being touched by their partner, fantasize, and can be orgasmic. Any of those things can happen.

BILL: So we always say, "An orgasm is an orgasm is an orgasm." No matter how it occurs, it doesn't have to be through intercourse only, it should be enjoyed.

COLIN: Did you get into that one where orgasms were not happening in the waking state?

CAROLYN: Yes. We also have to let people know that it's normal to be orgasmic when you're asleep. It's sort of a release valve, so that if the female doesn't have an orgasm while awake, Mother Nature looks after that, and she has an orgasmic response when she's asleep.

BILL: . . . And actually that question could apply to males as well. It doesn't have to be only females. They can have arousal during their sleeping hours . . . and of course, in the male, there may be an ejaculation that may occur . . . But it's normal for orgasms to occur during the night. Some people remember them, and some people don't.

CAROLYN: Now, why she's not having an orgasm when she's with her partner may be that this is a whole new experience for her, and she may not be aware of exactly what her needs are. She may be just beginning to be comfortable with her partner, and it may be something that will happen in the future, but at least she knows that everything is working okay physically because she is responsive when she's asleep.

BILL: So, it's very normal.

COLIN: Okay, let's move on here, and see how many questions we can get in. Here's another one. "Does it physically hurt a guy if he gets excited but doesn't get what he wants. My old boyfriend got really mad and said that a girl couldn't leave a guy excited like that."

CAROLYN: I love that one. We get that asked every time we do our talks.

(laughter)

BILL: Every time . . . and of course, the answer is absolutely no. There's no harmful effect whatsoever. That's probably the ultimate guilt that a male can dump on his girlfriend or his partner, and the only thing that he should see is two tire marks as she screeches her car and gets away from a guy like that . . . He's putting a tremendous amount of guilt on her, and she's going to end up with all kinds of problems if she goes ahead as a duty to him. It won't hurt him in any way, if he doesn't get what he wants.

CAROLYN: No. He won't die from a sperm embolism.

COLIN: Okay, let's move on to another question here. "Is it true that it takes longer for a female to reach orgasm than a male? That is, if he can only accomplish the act once, where does it leave the woman who also wants to reach an orgasm? Does she have to use other methods to reach satisfaction?"

CAROLYN: Okay, well, it may take the female longer, and it may not. It depends on the couple. In the beginning of the relationship, when they're both very young, the female may take longer to respond. As they get older, it may actually take the male longer to respond than the female but, definitely, she needs to look at other ways in which she can be responsive. She also needs to be an active participant, touching him as well as him touching her. If not, then what we get into are definite roadblocks. It's sort of like, "Look Ma, no hands." And that leads to more problems than anything else. She also needs to be at a fairly high level of arousal before they begin having intercourse.

BILL: Exactly. So, as an active participant, she can turn herself on, and then she can respond more quickly. Now the transition begins to occur as they age. Very often, it takes the male a little longer, as he ages, to have arousal and to reach an orgasm, but very often the female actually does speed up a little bit, so it can change throughout their life span, as they mature.

CAROLYN: And what we mean by, "She turns herself on," is touching, exploring her partner. That can increase her own level of arousal.

COLIN: How do you respond to the second part of that question, "If he can only accomplish the act once, where does it leave the woman who also wants to have an orgasm?"

BILL: Actually, that's a good question because . . . she has the potential to be responsive more than once . . . and be multi-orgasmic. Not every woman is, but she has the potential, so they need to use many other forms of stimulation.

CAROLYN: Yes. The female may be orgasmic before intercourse, with manual or oral stimulation, or she may be orgasmic with intercourse, or even afterwards, with manual or oral stimulation. All those are perfectly normal. We get into a lot of hangups with people feeling that it should be exactly the same for both partners.

COLIN: Okay, we'll move on to another question here, Bill and Carolyn. "What do you do when your partner wants a type of sex you don't want? Are you obligated to him even though it turns you off?"

CAROLYN: No.

(laughter)

BILL: The answer's a definite no. There should be no obligation for anyone, because then it becomes a sense of obligation rather than something that they enjoy together.

CAROLYN: I think this question could come from either sex . . . .

BILL: . . . Either person, that is.

CAROLYN: Yes. But what they need to say to their partner is, "This is what I like doing with you. I don't feel comfortable with that . . . but I enjoy doing other things." So what the partner needs to accept is, if there's a lot of other things that they really enjoy, to concentrate on those. The more pressure the other person gets, to do what they don't like, the more it's going to turn them off.

BILL: Each one of us has a different sexual value system, as to what is acceptable to us. We need to work within those guidelines, and if we put pressure on the partner who is not ready or is not interested in a particular experience, that creates all kinds of difficulties.

COLIN: Yes, as we discussed a few weeks ago, sex should never be an obligation, should it?

BILL: . . . That's exactly right.

CAROLYN: Yes, if it becomes an obligation, he or she could end up feeling, "I never want to have sex with this person again."

COLIN: Okay, let's move on to another question here. "My girlfriend doesn't consider sex really important. She usually has an orgasm but still doesn't like sex. What am I doing wrong?"

BILL: Well, he's probably not doing very much wrong.

(laughter)

CAROLYN: What we have to look at here . . . she may just have a different desire level, Colin. There also may be some conflicts in the relationship. You have to look at, "What's the communication like? Are there power struggles going on? Is there hostility?" All these things need to be looked at. It also reminds me of a cartoon that I saw recently. It had a peacock, a male peacock, strutting his feathers, iridescent, glowing in the sunlight. He was strutting in front of the female peacock, and she looked very disinterested. The caption at the bottom said, "What do you mean? No."

(laughter)

BILL: Exactly. There may also be differences in what their expectations are. It sounds like, from the question, he's putting the emphasis on intercourse and orgasm. She may have other needs, like more closeness and intimacy. It sounds like she's responsive, because she's having an orgasm, but he thinks her desire level should be the same as his . . . and so he's putting a lot of pressure on her. He's probably not doing anything physically wrong.

CAROLYN: No, the problem here is, he's looking at the situation as if he's going to be her coach.

BILL: Right.

CAROLYN: She doesn't need a coach. She needs to find out if this is meeting her needs. It's okay. If she feels she wants to have more sexual activity, it should be up to her.

COLIN: Well, Carolyn, Bill, you get lots and lots of interesting questions. It must be a fascinating type of group to address.

CAROLYN: It's always surprising, because we never know what questions we're going to get, and the questions are very legitimate and really interesting.

BILL: And they're just a fascinating age group, because they're so keen on wanting to know everything . . . and not afraid to ask.

COLIN: Bill, Carolyn, thanks very much.

CAROLYN: Good, thanks, Colin.

BILL: Thanks, it's been a pleasure.

QUOTES FROM COUPLES

These comments come from a young male partner:
When I touch her gentiles, nothing happens.
I'm a very viral guy.
She just can't seem to reach an organism.

I got my sex education from a tampon box.

LOVERS AND OTHER STRANGERS

COLIN GREWAR: 'Tis the wedding season. Thousands of glowing men and women will meet at the altar this spring, looking forward to a long and happy life together. Sadly, what starts out as a wonderful relationship often deteriorates. Three or four years later our loving couple is living together, but just barely. They act more like roommates than husband and wife. Lovers and Other Strangers is the topic of our relationships column this week. Joining me now are Dr. Bill and Carolyn Chernenkoff, co-therapists in marital and sexual counselling in Saskatoon. Good Afternoon, Carolyn, Bill.

CAROLYN: Hello, Colin.

BILL: Hi, Colin.

COLIN: So what are some of the common signs of a marriage in which the husband and wife seem to be strangers?

CAROLYN: This is something that we're seeing fairly often.

BILL: We see at least one couple per week who fit this pattern almost identically. There are a lot of people with this problem.

CAROLYN: Yes, there are. Usually they are a couple in their midtwenties. They usually have been married about three or four years, and they started out with a wonderful relationship. This is the person each of them wanted to spend the rest of their lives with . . .

BILL: And now it's three or four years later. Suddenly they realize there's no sharing of anything, time or emotions. Actually, they feel an indifference toward one another. It's just as if they were roommates living together, with sex thrown in once in a while.

CAROLYN: Uh huuh.

BILL: And then suddenly one or both of them say, "I might as well be on my own. I want a divorce." It suddenly jumps from only three years ago when they wanted to be together forever, to now, divorce. There are a number of things that have happened to lead to that situation.

COLIN: Yes, what happened along the way?

CAROLYN: We have brought in different ideas from the couples that we have been seeing. And we'll paint a picture of what may be happening along parallel lines with her life and with his life. In her life, she works full time or part time, and she's totally responsible for the family and the home.

BILL: He has a full-time job. He spends long hours working, and he really doesn't have any time for the home or the family.

CAROLYN: And she likes nice things. She has a big house and a new car, and she expects him to provide these things for her.

BILL: He takes on extra jobs. Sometimes these jobs are in the evenings and sometimes on the weekends. He feels that if he works hard and if he buys nice things, they'll all be happy. But there's no time for him to be at home.

CAROLYN: And she's not really concerned about the finances. Somehow it'll just all work out.

BILL: But he's worried about money all the time, and yet, basically, they're fairly well set financially.

CAROLYN: Yes, and she is a clean queen. She has an immaculate house . . . *(laughter)* . . . she works very hard during the day, then she comes home and spends her spare time cleaning the house.

BILL: He doesn't have any desire or time to be at home. He spends long hours away from home, and he loves his work. That's a common thing that we hear people saying, " I love my work."

CAROLYN: She keeps all her feelings inside, but when he comes home, she lets him know when she's angry. She starts slamming the cupboard doors. She gives him the cold, silent treatment.

BILL: And he doesn't share any of his feelings. In fact, he belittles her or puts her down. Often we hear him saying things like, "You're wrong," or "That's stupid."

CAROLYN: Yes. And she spends all of her leisure time with the children or her girlfriends. They have no holiday time together. They have no leisure time together.

BILL: He spends his leisure time with his buddies. He just loves hunting and fishing, as the male partners often tell us. He says to her, "My buddies think I'm a prince of a guy."

CAROLYN: And she says, "They don't know you."

(laughter)

BILL: Do you notice what pattern weaves through all this?

COLIN: Well, they seem to have wonderful full lives, except they don't seem to care the least bit about each other.

BILL: Exactly, Colin.

CAROLYN: . . . And then they say, "We've drifted apart." They obviously have when you look at what's happening to them. They do nothing together. They're running on parallel lines. What happens very often, is that one or both will say, "I might as well be on my own. I have a full life, but it's just for me, and so why should I be with this other person? I might as well have a divorce."

BILL: Each of them develops a protective indifference. There's no joy or fun in being together for this couple.

COLIN: And it's certainly the fault of both of them. It takes two . . .

CAROLYN: Yes, you can see how it meshes.

BILL: . . . Yes, where they used to be lovers who really cared for each other, now they've really become strangers. They are closer to the other people around them than to each other.

CAROLYN: Right. Actually, that's what we do see, Colin, it is not that this couple really hate one another.

BILL: No.

CAROLYN: They still have commitment, they still care for one another, but it's buried, by the lifestyle they have. Really, they are victims of their environment and the pressures that they're going through. The priority of the relationship is at the very bottom of the scale. Everything else comes first.

COLIN: So, supposing we have a couple that's reached this stage. Is there anything they can do to save the marriage?

BILL: Yes, there sure is.

CAROLYN: Yes, yes.

BILL: Anyone hearing this and feeling that they're somewhere in this picture . . . If this is familiar . . . a little red light should go on. They should look at what's happening to them. They need to look at their priorities, such as – "Can we do with less?"

CAROLYN: Uh huhhh.

BILL: . . . Because, obviously, he's working harder and harder to provide material things.

CAROLYN: And, of course, when he's working harder and harder to provide these things, she's angry at him, because he's not at home helping with the family. That's one of the things that they need to look at immediately. They also have to look at her attitude about "everything will work out financially" and putting the total onus on him. First of all, they have to sit down and look at, "What are our goals, where are we going with this?"

BILL: We recommend very highly that every couple, after they get married, every six to twelve months, should sit down and have a reassessment. They should actually write down: "what are our objectives? Is this what we want to do? are we accomplishing – perhaps financially – what we want to do? What is happening in our relationship?"

CAROLYN: Yes. Exactly, another thing to look at is: "are we able to spend some time together? If he's working at fewer jobs, and maybe the house doesn't have to be quite so clean, we'll have a little bit of time that we can spend together as a family, and also time for just the two of us to be together."

BILL: Maybe one room could be immaculate *(laughter)*, the living room. The rest may not have to be quite as clean.

CAROLYN: Right, what happens now is that when he does come home, she's after him all the time, "How come you're not vacuuming, how come you're not cleaning?" So even when they are together, it's not a pleasurable situation. What they need to look at is, "Where can we take time out of tasks, and put it into time for just the two of us?" We recommend that at least every three to six months, they have one weekend that they go away somewhere, just the two of them, have some time together, recharge the batteries.

BILL: Now that, Colin, is something we recommend for couples even if they don't have problems – have not become strangers. Every couple needs to be able to have R & R time, to recuperate, to be able to recharge themselves, just to go to a hotel, or overnight somewhere together. . . .

CAROLYN: . . . It could be camping . . .

BILL: . . . Yes, or camping, for example, is what some people choose. But they should get away from everybody else. That's really an essential ingredient.

COLIN: And I guess it would help to have hobbies, maybe try to find one together. The couple you described – he liked hunting and she liked, being with the girls, so maybe they should look for something they can do together.

CAROLYN: Exactly, and this having separate interests often evolves with neither person intending it to happen, it's just the circumstances. This couple don't need to get a divorce. If they can get back on track, they can actually have a very committed relationship, but they have to put some energy into the relationship.

BILL: There's great potential, because they've only been married for three or four years. This is a couple who really cared for each other. They can become lovers again, and not be strangers.

COLIN: In the introduction I, mentioned that a lot of people are getting married right now. I guess, this is a problem that you should start trying to avoid the day you get married.

CAROLYN: Yes, yes.

COLIN: Because I can really see it becoming a trap for young couples that are trying to get ahead and establish some financial base.

CAROLYN: Exactly, and you can't put the relationship on hold, because if you do, it may not be there when you want to bring it back.

(laughter)

BILL: They need to start assessing where they're at, right from the beginning, every six to twelve months. Every three months they should try to get away just by themselves, but every six to twelve months they should sit down and actually take an inventory of their relationship, not only an inventory of their financial status.

COLIN: Okay, Carolyn, Bill, thank you very much.

CAROLYN: Okay, thanks, Colin.

BILL: A pleasure.

LONG-DISTANCE RELATIONSHIPS

COLIN GREWAR: Balancing a career with a happy love life seems to be getting more and more difficult in the modern, working world. One of the stresses many couples are now facing is the long-distance relationship, where employment requirements take one of the partners away from home for long periods of time. Joining me now to talk about this are Bill and Carolyn Chernenkoff, co-therapists in marital and sexual counselling in Saskatoon. Hello, Carolyn, Bill.

CAROLYN: Hi, Colin.

BILL: Hi, good afternoon, Colin.

COLIN: What kinds of situations are the most vulnerable to the stresses of one of these long-distance relationships?

CAROLYN: Well, certainly, Colin, if the partners are separated for long periods of time, we call it a "suitcase marriage." Traditionally, it was the male that was away from home for long periods of time, and he would come home just on weekends. But we're seeing more frequently now where it's the female who is employed away from the family home. It may be a young woman who just graduated and perhaps she has to get a teaching job away from the city, or else a woman who is a minister, who's living in a small town somewhere in Saskatchewan, and she's commuting back and forth.

BILL: Or business people who are basically on the road.

CAROLYN: On the road again.

BILL: Exactly. This is becoming more and more common, and so, as a consequence, they really end up living single in a double bed.

COLIN: Sounds like the name of a song, Bill.

(laughter)

CAROLYN: Yes, doesn't it, Colin.

COLIN: Is the situation more difficult for the partner that's away or for the one that stays home?

BILL: Well, it's actually difficult for both.

CAROLYN: Well, I would say it's usually more difficult for the partner who is away.

BILL: I guess I agree with Carolyn . . . what happens is that the person who is away probably has a more difficult time of it.

CAROLYN: . . . Because the one who's at home feels more secure. She has the home and the children . . . and the other one is almost like an outsider, like a guest.

BILL: . . . And he doesn't know where he fits in sometimes. The away partner expects this overwhelming warmth of appreciation for coming home, and doesn't always receive it.

(laughter)

COLIN: So, the problems are, I guess, exacerbated when they're together, rather than when they're apart.

CAROLYN: Yes, yes.

BILL: Exactly. It's quite common for people to have a conflict or an argument as soon as the partner that's away gets home.

CAROLYN: Right.

BILL: . . . Let's listen to Joe and Ann present a typical scenario.

CAROLYN: Okay, Joe has been away all week. He arrives home Friday night, and about two hours later, he hears this from Ann . . .

ANN: "You've been home for two hours. You were away all week. You were staying in hotels and had a really nice time. You come home and you act like a guest. You just sit on the chesterfield and give orders and expect to be waited on."

JOE: "Well Ann, you ignore me. I mean, I give you directions about what you're supposed to do, it's just as simple as that. If you'd just follow them, there really wouldn't be any problem."

ANN: "When did you say you were leaving again?"

(laughter)

COLIN: Hardly the warm welcome. So things can get kind of nasty when one partner returns.

CAROLYN: Yes, the final cutting edge.

COLIN: What about when that partner leaves again, or . . .

CAROLYN: Those are the two parts, Colin, right there, where the feelings come to a critical crossroad. First of all, there's often a feeling of closeness before they part, and then there might be a confrontation just before the separation. It's like a type of separation anxiety. Unconsciously, the partner at home may feel, "If I don't get too close, and maybe if I distance myself at the end, and maybe if I'm angry at my partner, I won't miss him so much."

BILL: But, in actuality, that creates a whole set of new emotions when the one partner is away, because of the difficulty when they parted. They experience nagging emotions of guilt for a week or ten days when they are not together because the time when they were together did not end very constructively.

CAROLYN: Right, and then when they are reunited, usually the partner away is really looking forward to coming home and the partner at home is also anticipating the reunion. Initially, they're very excited, but underneath there's an emotional feeling and a memory of being hurt the last time, "Why did he leave me? Why did I get left with all these jobs, all this responsibility?" Some

resentment is there as well. So often there's also an initial confrontation when he first gets home.

BILL: It's as if the adult in us feels . . . "Gee, I'm looking forward
to seeing my partner." But the child in us feels, "I was deserted . . .
he left me."

CAROLYN: Yes, "he deserted me."

(laughter)

BILL: Exactly. Those are normal feelings. What's important is
that the couple identify what's happening and what to do about it.
That's the key.

COLIN: So, what would make the homecoming a bit healthier for
the relationship?

BILL: Well, if we have a look at Ann and Joe again . . .

CAROLYN: Okay. Ann and Joe had a confrontation Friday night.
This relationship is sinking fast. It's going downhill. They only
have Friday, Saturday and Sunday before he leaves again. What
they need to look at is – we've got to solve this pretty quickly. We
have to get rid of all the trivia and get down to the nitty gritty.

BILL: . . . So now Ann may approach it a little differently.

CAROLYN: . . . She needs to express her true feelings . . .

ANN: "Joe, I think I've done a pretty good job of looking after the
household responsibilities and the children when you were away. I
get really frustrated when you come home and start giving all these
directions about what I should have done differently."

JOE: "Well, you know, Ann, I think you actually do manage well. I
guess that's where I feel that . . . I'm left out, when I'm away.
When I come back, I start giving instruction and orders to everybody to sort of be part of the whole scene again, the family structure. But, I do want you to know that, when I'm on the road and
I'm away, it's not a fun time for me. It's actually hard work for me

when I'm away, but anyway, I'm glad I'm home and I'm glad I'm home with you and the children."

ANN: "Okay Joe, I understand. Actually – it may look like I did pretty well, but this is sort of after the dust has cleared. I've had a really hard week. It was one crisis after another, and I'd like to go out for a coffee and just talk it over with you."

JOE: "I'd like that, Ann."

ANN: "Okay Joe, I'm ready to go."

COLIN: It sounds like this is going to be a much more enjoyable weekend.

CAROLYN: Yes, Colin, yes.

BILL: They've turned it around and instead of blaming each other and one cutting the other down . . .

(laughter)

CAROLYN: Yes.

BILL: . . . Right at the knees, so to speak, they're getting their feelings out, and they're quite different, aren't they. They're negotiating a little bit of time for each other. And, you notice, they are creating an environment which is more neutral. That's a very constructive thing for people to do, preplan something, a social event, or going out to eat at a restaurant, so that they can get sort of reacquainted again in a more neutral place.

COLIN: What are some other things that couples should do, maybe when they're apart, to keep that long-distance relationship a bit healthier?

BILL: Well, I think that what you raise is really important. First of all, the remain-at-home spouse should have a career or do something that is fulfilling.

CAROLYN: Yes, it may be looking after family, whatever the person at home feels is rewarding and satisfying for them. If he or she is left at home waiting anxiously for the other person to come back, and light up their life, it's going to be a very depressing week. What they need to do is find things that are really interesting and satisfying for themselves.

BILL: If the remain-at-home spouse is emotionally dependent on the away-from-home spouse, to come home and meet all the emotional needs, a lot of frustration will surface.

CAROLYN: One of the other things they need to do is use the telephone . . . just to get in touch with the other person, just to hear each other's voices.

BILL: You know that commercial – *Reach out and touch someone* – it has a ring of truth to it.

(laughter)

BILL: . . . They need to budget how much they spend on telephone calls, because it's not the fact of what you say, it's the fact of hearing the voice. In fact, there shouldn't be heavy duty things discussed on the phone. It should just be a fun communication.

CAROLYN: Right, you don't want to tell your partner when he phones and is across the ocean somewhere, "Well, you know, the dog just ate one of your best shoes."

CAROLYN: Because what are they going to do about the situation . . . They should just discuss how things are going, be fairly up and positive. Also, what they need to do, before they separate, is look at how they're going to delineate their roles, so the person at home doesn't feel that she has the responsibility to do everything. Then when the other person comes home, resentment about being responsible for everything is not there.

BILL: And the away-from-home spouse knows that he's not left out, and can immediately take over some role that is designated for him. Those are constructive things to do.

COLIN: Would you advise, Bill and Carolyn, maybe taking the partner along on the occasional work trip.

BILL: Now that's a good thing . . .

CAROLYN: Yes, Colin.

BILL: From time to time, the stay-at-home partner should go with the suitcase partner.

CAROLYN: The reason for that, Colin, is that when one person is away, the one at home thinks that even though he's away at a meeting or a training course, he's on vacation.

(laughter)

BILL: And he's not.

CAROLYN: No, it's important for the stay-at-home spouse to go and see what the suitcase spouse really does. We have heard of couples where the husband owns his own truck, and he takes his wife on a run with him once a month, just to have time with her. We've also heard of situations where the wife is away working, teaching in a small town. When the husband has a slack period, he stays with his wife in the small town for a couple of weeks.

BILL: Those are very constructive suggestions. If a couple learns to use some of these, basically what ends up occurring is, in a way, lots of mini re-acquaintances and lots of mini honeymoons.

CAROLYN: It takes a lot of energy, but it certainly can work.

BILL: Yes.

COLIN: Okay, Bill, Carolyn, thank you very much.

CAROLYN: Good, thanks, Colin.

BILL: A pleasure.

QUOTES FROM COUPLES

I don't know what would happen if we went on a trip together, because I don't know if we would ever find anything to do together.

DO I HAVE TO GO TO YOUR STAFF CHRISTMAS PARTY?

COLIN GREWAR: 'Tis the season to be jolly, and that means it's time for the staff Christmas party, but you know, it doesn't always turn out to be such a great time. It can be a source of conflict for a normally happy couple. To tell us more, I'm joined by Dr. Bill and Carolyn Chernenkoff, co-therapists in marital and sexual counselling. Hello, Bill, Carolyn.

CAROLYN: Hi, Colin.

BILL: Hi, Colin.

COLIN: Now, you know, this is supposed to be a fun event, the staff Christmas party, in the true spirit of the season. What happens? Why do so many staff Christmas parties turn out to be so miserable for so many?

CAROLYN: Well, I think one of the reasons, Colin, is that it only occurs once a year. Very often the spouses who aren't on staff, and are going with their partners, feel very awkward. They feel they don't have anything in common with the people at the office. They feel shy and embarrassed, and it's not always an enjoyable time.

BILL: Exactly, and this is one of the areas where the male still has a pretty high expectation that his spouse, his wife, will go to his Christmas party.

CAROLYN: Uh huhhh, although it does happen on both sides, because of course, in the majority of families now, both husband and wife are working.

BILL: Right, and so it can be distressful in either direction. We have a couple called Bob and Alice who can maybe illustrate the problem.

COLIN: Okay.

BILL: Bob comes home from work, and says . . .

BOB: "Alice, the Christmas party is at 7:00 o'clock this Friday. We have to be there on time so get a babysitter so we can go."

ALICE: "It's coming so quickly this year. I thought maybe they'd cancel it or something."

BOB: "Yeah, no, we have to be there at 7:00 o'clock."

ALICE: "And I have to be there?"

BOB: "Yes, of course, the spouses are expected to be there."

ALICE: "I suppose if I didn't go, you'd lose your job."

BOB: "Well, that's not the point, but I know we have to be there at 7:00 o'clock."

COLIN: Ummm, that doesn't sound like a very nice invitation . . .

(laughter)

CAROLYN: And by the way, get a babysitter too.

BILL: Yes, exactly, as if that's her job . . . her responsibility.

CAROLYN: Yes.

BILL: And yet, Colin, this is a very common approach for a lot of people.

CAROLYN: Uh huhhh.

BILL: As if it's just expected.

CAROLYN: The expectation is there, whether she wants to go or not, she should be there. There's no choice. As the "good wife," she should be there.

BILL: Consequently, when they leave the Christmas party, you can cut the tension with a knife . . .

CAROLYN: . . . What happens is that she can't get mad at the people who are at the party. She may feel awkward and very embarrassed. She may spend the whole evening standing by the food table or sitting in a chair holding up the wall at the back of the room, but she's nice to everyone and very polite. Then she gets in the car on the way home, and bang.

BOB: "You sure didn't have a very good time."

ALICE: "Well, you took off like a shot and you didn't spend any time with me. You were with your buddies the whole night." . . .

BOB: "Well, you didn't circulate, you just didn't mingle at all."

ALICE: . . . "You were just awful, you neglected me."

BOB: "Oh, sure."

(laughter)

COLIN: And then they go home and . . . turn their backs on each other. It's a tense weekend all around.

CAROLYN: That's about it. It goes on for the whole weekend and neither one feels good about the situation. They're also left with very negative feelings about the next year.

BILL: Exactly, but it doesn't have to be that way, Colin.

COLIN: Yes, I guess so – maybe if we could back up, it probably starts with Bob's approach.

CAROLYN: Yes.

BILL: Okay, now suppose Bob comes home. He's just found out that the Christmas party is on this Friday. He can approach it differently. He can say . . .

BOB: "Alice, the Christmas party is this Friday. I didn't find out about it until now. I know it's been tense for us in the past, but I'd like to invite you to come."

ALICE: "An invitation!"

BOB: "Yes."

ALICE: "That's wonderful. However, I'd like to share something about the Christmas party with you. I have always felt awkward at those parties. I'm very shy and I have difficulty meeting people; it's hard for me; and I have felt very embarrassed and really had a miserable time every year. I feel very much alone, and isolated, and what usually happens is that on the way home in the car, I blow up, and I pick a fight with you."

BOB: "I know. I remember those times, but anyway, my life doesn't depend on it. My job doesn't depend on it. If you'd like to come, I'd love to have you come with me."

ALICE: "Okay. I would like to go, but I would also like to be able to spend more time with you at the Christmas party."

BOB: "I'd like that."

ALICE: "Okay, and I'd also like us to be able to agree that we can leave maybe at 11:00 o'clock, 11:30 – early, so I don't feel like it's going on forever."

BOB: "Oh, no problem with that."

ALICE: "Okay, and I'd also like to invite you to go out, just the two of us, the next night, Saturday night."

BOB: "Terrific."

ALICE: "The two of us together."

COLIN: Ah, that way they can talk over the Christmas party. So she sort of sets the ground rules then.

(laughter)

CAROLYN: Yes.

BILL: Exactly.

CAROLYN: Yes, because actually, she's going as a guest. It is his Christmas party, the staff Christmas party. He's inviting her, and it's something that she doesn't really feel comfortable with. With the second approach she gets some input. She can say, "This is how I would feel more comfortable, if this is how it could be handled."

BILL: And it's his responsibility to make sure that she feels comfortable at the party – to be with her, to introduce her, to mingle with her, rather than going off with the boys and leaving her by herself.

CAROLYN: Right, and of course, what often happens is that the employees feel very comfortable with all their co-workers, so the minute they get into the room, they take off like a shot. They never introduce their partners to anybody else on the staff, and it can be a miserable evening for their partners.

COLIN: All the spouses who don't know each other are sort of left sitting, they're scattered about the room and feeling uncomfortable.

CAROLYN: Yes, yes, exactly.

BILL: Yes, sitting stiffly in their chairs.

(laughter)

COLIN: Bill and Carolyn, if it is such a horrible experience for a spouse, what if he or she really doesn't want to go?

BILL: That's really important, Colin.

CAROLYN: That's right, Colin. Those feelings also need to be respected, so if Bob invited Alice and she really didn't want to go, she could say . . .

BOB: "Well, Alice, the party is on at 7:00 o'clock this Friday, and I'd really like to have you come."

ALICE: "Okay, I have to be very honest with you. The staff Christmas party is probably one of the most stressful times I've ever had. I don't look forward to going to that party, and I would really prefer not to be there."

BOB: "Well, I can understand that. I'll miss you."

ALICE: "Okay."

BOB: "Okay, but even though I understand, it's a tense situation. I sort of feel obligated to go, because it is my work."

ALICE: " I can understand your position."

BOB: "But my job doesn't depend on you being there, at least it's not in the contract."

ALICE: "Okay."

BOB: "And so what I'll do is, I'll go, but I'll come home earlier, and spend the rest of the evening with you."

ALICE: "That makes me feel much better."

CAROLYN: So, the end result is – it doesn't have to be a power struggle where one person says, "You've got to go," and the other one says, "No, I won't." With the last two discussions we've outlined, each partner's feelings are quite different. Alice can say, "I don't feel that I can get into that situation. When my feelings are accepted by my partner, I feel really good about him because of that."

BILL: You see, they're much more likely to have fun together afterwards.

CAROLYN: And it's much more likely she'll be greeting him quite happily at the door when he comes home.

(laughter)

COLIN: Instead of storming to the door ahead of him while he puts the car away.

BILL: Exactly.

CAROLYN: Right, that's right.

COLIN: He shouldn't insist on it, ever.

CAROLYN: No, no, not ever, even though he may get a lot of pressure from co-workers. And very often it's with the idea of – you bring your spouse or your girlfriend around, because we want to check her out. We want to see what she's like. And of course, that's not usually an enjoyable situation.

BILL: No, it's an uncomfortable situation for the spouse, because she's just there to be examined visually, so to speak.

(laughter)

COLIN: Yes, but on the other hand . . . it might put him in a bit of an uncomfortable situation as he's told all his fellow workers about his girlfriend. When he shows up, and she's not by his side, and they ask why? Does he say, "Well, you know, she really hates all of you."

(laughter)

BILL: No Colin, but he's got to turn it into a positive then. He's got to say, "You know, she's wonderful. She's busy tonight and couldn't make it, but gee, fellows, that's why I have to leave at 10:30.

(laughter)

BILL: Because I'm looking forward to being with her.

CAROLYN: Yes.

BILL: And he turns it into a positive – this is somebody so special for him that he wants to get home earlier to be with her. Rather than saying, "Well, you're right, she's a real wallflower and she didn't want to come, and so I came by myself." Because then he's being taken advantage of by his co-workers.

CAROLYN: What we see happening more commonly is – if it's women who are working, and their spouses or their partners prefer not to come, they will very often go with a group from the office to the staff Christmas party and have a good time that way.

COLIN: We've been talking about the Christmas party, but this probably applies all through the year to office functions.

CAROLYN: Yes.

BILL: The same scenario.

CAROLYN: Yes, it does, Colin, because it's a unique situation. These are people that you are working with all the time, but socially you may not have that much in common with them. It's quite a different circumstance when you see them socially, so if it doesn't work out, don't be concerned. You can still enjoy working with them professionally.

BILL: Exactly, and it does occur regularly in other areas as well.

CAROLYN: Yes, your spouse may play on a baseball or hockey team or in a musical group. The same applies to get-togethers with any outside group.

COLIN: Okay, Bill and Carolyn, what sort of a Christmas party do you guys have?

BILL: Well actually, we have tried over the years having a staff dinner, sometimes going out and sometimes going to various homes, and that's worked out okay. It isn't something that all the spouses of the staff want to attend, and as we discussed now, that's okay too. This year we're doing something different . . .

CAROLYN: . . . This year what we're doing is taking all the staff out for lunch, and then we're giving them Christmas Eve afternoon off, so they can spend the time with their families, which I think may be more enjoyable.

(laughter)

BILL: . . . More enjoyable than being with us.

COLIN: The spouses will appreciate that.

CAROLYN: I think so too.

BILL: Exactly.

CAROLYN: And the staff seem to be very appreciative. They're looking forward to it as well.

COLIN: Well, Bill, Carolyn, this is the last time we'll talk before Christmas, so I hope you both have a very festive and happy time.

CAROLYN: Thank you very much, Colin.

BILL: We'd like to wish you and all the listeners a very happy Christmas.

CAROLYN: And we hope that all the Christmas gatherings are pleasant and enjoyable.

BILL: And a real pleasure.

QUOTES FROM COUPLES

We had intercourse at Christmas time and on my birthday.

*He would ejaculate and lie there
as if he had died . . . and fall asleep.*

LIVING WITH A DIFFICULT MAN OR WOMAN

COLIN GREWAR: We all know certain people who we describe as moody. They can be sweet and nice as pie one day, and angry, mean and cranky the next. Getting along with this type of person can be difficult, and if you happen to live with one, it can really test a relationship. Bill and Carolyn Chernenkoff are co-therapists in marital and sexual counselling in Saskatoon. They join me today to talk about living with a difficult man or woman. Good afternoon, Carolyn, Bill.

BILL: Good afternoon, Colin.

CAROLYN: Hello, Colin.

COLIN: So what are some of the most common characteristics of a difficult person in a relationship?

(laughter)

CAROLYN: Well, Colin, just as you said in the introduction, this person has black moods. These black moods can go on for long periods of time. They may also have long periods of silence as well, where they don't talk to their partner for days and even weeks.

BILL: It may be a sort of brooding silence at times. It can be a mixture of various things. One of the things that may be present is temper tantrums, for example. It may be a very explosive display of temper at times.

CAROLYN: For unrealistic reasons.

BILL: These people can be demanding. They can be controlling, for example, and sometimes very intimidating.

CAROLYN: Yes.

COLIN: Would these be characteristics that are confined to their relationships with their partners or would these people be difficult and demanding all the time?

CAROLYN: Well actually, Colin, that's a good question. That's where it is clear that this is a difficult person. The mood swings are almost under his control. He may be very silent and controlling to his partner, but as soon as the phone rings and a friend is on the other end of the line, he becomes very friendly and jovial, a wonderful person. Then he hangs up the phone and again, the silent, controlling behavior is there.

BILL: And that's a differentiating feature, Colin. These people can be cruel one moment and be charming the next moment.

CAROLYN: Uh huhhh.

BILL: It's quite different from the person who is depressed all the time, because that can be a clinical problem, a depression.

CAROLYN: Where the person is blue or sad all the time . . .

BILL: . . . The difficult person is one who can change back and forth, almost at will. It's a controllable situation.

CAROLYN: Yes. And it goes in both directions. We see it on both sides, the difficult person may be a male or a female. It's not just confined to one sex.

BILL: We used to, when we first started counselling, – think it was the male who tended to be the difficult one, but we have found it to be quite otherwise. We see instances where either partner can be difficult.

COLIN: Well, it must make living together very difficult.

BILL: Yes.

CAROLYN: Yes, yes, it does.

BILL: If we have a look at a little scenario, this will give us some idea of what we mean by this type of difficult person. We now meet Donna and Ken.

CAROLYN: It's the end of the day, and Donna sees Ken driving up the driveway. He opens the front door and she says . . .

DONNA: "How was your day?"

KEN: "What are you doing, writing a book? I don't have to explain what my day was like to you."

CAROLYN: Now Donna becomes silent. She knows that this is the beginning of an awful evening. So what she does is – and this is what we've often heard women say – "I put his supper on the table and I go and sit in the bedroom."

BILL: Now, can you feel the intimidation that's occurring in that situation?

COLIN: Yes.

BILL: Right. Now this is a very difficult person to live with . . .

CAROLYN: Yes. There's a very black cloud hanging over them.

BILL: . . . Especially if they go on and on. Now, we mean, Colin, all of us have times when we're not nice. We have bad moments, but this is a person whose bad moments with his partner are continuous.

COLIN: This is happening a lot.

CAROLYN: A lot. It perpetuates the tension through the whole evening, through many days and many weeks. The person living with the difficult individual is walking on eggshells. She's sort of – we describe it as being the individual's human mood ring. Remember when people had mood rings, which indicated what kind of mood they were in. She's always testing to see, "Is he going to be in a good mood? Is he going to be in a bad mood?" She doesn't want to say anything that might upset him.

COLIN: How about the sexual relationship between this couple?

CAROLYN: . . . Well, what ends up happening, Colin, is that the female feels that she cannot respond to her partner. But, very often, she is afraid to say to him, "I don't want to go ahead." So she will cooperate sexually through a sense of obligation and duty. She will feel used and exploited and then develop resentment and hostility herself. But she tends to keep it all inside; she's afraid if she does say anything, it's going to rock the boat even more.

BILL: Now this is where there's a slight difference between males and females. If it is the male who is the difficult person, generally, along with the other demands, there are sexual demands as well. And you can imagine, if he says, "Well, I have a right, you have to provide sex for me." You can imagine how aroused she's going to become in that situation. It's not very likely.

CAROLYN: No.

BILL: Now, if it's the other way around, if it's the female who is demanding, it's very interesting. Usually she won't be demanding sexually. But what happens is that the male, who is the affected partner, just doesn't feel close to the female.

CAROLYN: No, usually she doesn't want to have sex with him at all. We had one woman recently who was a difficult person. She said to her partner, "You've had enough sex for your whole life, so you don't get any more."

BILL: Yes, she controls him by willfully withholding sex.

COLIN: It must be very difficult because the person who's not the difficult person must be wondering all the time, "Why is my partner like this?"

CAROLYN: That's right, Colin.

BILL: That's the effect it begins to have. The partner who is affected begins to feel, "Is it me? What am I doing wrong?"

CAROLYN: And he or she feels, "Maybe if I were a better wife, or if I were a better husband, or if I were able to make sure that these problems didn't arise, I could prevent my partner from having these blue moods."

BILL: And when we're taking histories from couples like this, we ask, "Is your work affecting your relationship?" They often say, "No, it's just the reverse. My relationship affects my work. I feel so uncomfortable and knotted up when I go to work, I can't concentrate at work."

CAROLYN: Uh huhhh.

BILL: That's how it affects them, not only in their personal lives, but in their professional lives as well.

COLIN: So, Bill, Carolyn, can we salvage a relationship like this? Is there any way to deal with it?

CAROLYN: Well, actually, there are things that need to be done, and can be done. First of all, if it is the female, who is living with the difficult person – what she needs to look at is, "How important is this relationship to me?" Basically she has three choices.

BILL: **The first choice is the status quo**, and basically that is – if she feels that she wants to preserve that relationship at all costs, that no matter how difficult her partner is, she wants them to remain together, and she just puts up with it. That's the status quo.

CAROLYN: Right. **The second choice is to have separate futures**, meaning that she can say to her partner, "I care for you, and I love you, but I am being emotionally destroyed. I'm a wreck. If there are no changes that are going to occur in this relationship, I can no longer continue to live with you."

BILL: Now, in order to do that, she has to begin developing some independence.

CAROLYN: Yes.

BILL: Meaning that she has to be able to have something that she can fall back on, and she has to mean it. This is a really essential key, Colin, because the difficult person has almost a sixth sense. He knows whether his partner is serious or not. And if the difficult person has any perception that this is not really a serious threat, he will just keep right on, and he won't make any changes at all.

CAROLYN: Now, interestingly enough, when one person gives an ultimatum, and the other individual realizes that the relationship is actually in jeopardy, that the partner is not going to continue to stay in the relationship, that may initiate some change. So **the third choice is to get some help** – for them to seek professional help together.

BILL: It's not unusual for us to see one person first because one partner refuses to come in, and, as you can imagine, it's not the difficult person who comes in and says, "I'm a difficult person." It's the other partner who comes in and says, "Look, this is what's happening to me. I'm being destroyed by this." We encourage people to seek whatever help they have in their area. All they need is to have a reaffirmation, by the agency or the service, that it is okay to seek help. Each person has the right to say, "I'm being affected by this. I can't remain in this relationship as it is."

CAROLYN: Actually, it is very interesting, we have seen couples where the woman initiates coming for help, and then, when she confronts her partner, he does come in as well. When he does have the motivation to change, he can be effective in making changes. They can continue to be in a relationship which is rewarding for both of them after they put energy into rebuilding the relationship and learning effective communication skills.

BILL: They can make dramatic changes, and it's really delightful to see this occur.

CAROLYN: Yes.

COLIN: Okay, Bill, Carolyn, thanks very much.

CAROLYN: Thank you, Colin.

BILL: A pleasure.

QUOTES FROM COUPLES

Male partner to female partner –
"Imagine if after all this counselling we were to find out you are really a nice person after all."

I hope there isn't a charge for counselling, because I want to get my cat fixed.

You can overdose on those self-help books.

WHEN YOUR PARTNER HAS AN AFFAIR WITH YOUR BEST FRIEND

COLIN GREWAR: It's a crushing blow to find out your spouse or partner is having an affair. The situation becomes even worse if he or she is having that affair with your best friend. It's not just the stuff of soap operas, you know. It happens a lot. Joining me now to talk about it are Bill and Carolyn Chernenkoff, co-therapists in marital and sexual counselling in Saskatoon. Hi, Carolyn, Bill.

CAROLYN: Hi, Colin.

BILL: Hi, Colin.

COLIN: How does this happen?

BILL: It brings to mind a scenario which we've probably all heard in some form or other. The man says, "A terrible thing happened to me. My wife ran away with my best friend. You know, I really miss my best friend."

(laughter)

BILL: You see . . . what happens is the double whammie.

COLIN: Yes.

CAROLYN: Right, Colin, sometimes, if the relationship has not been a good one, the person isn't sure, "Who am I going to miss most, my best friend or my spouse?" How does it happen? Well, usually, these are couples who've done a lot of things together. They go on holidays together. They go out socially together. They go to the lake together, and you begin to see that your husband actually is having more fun with your best friend. They seem to be the ones who go in swimming together. They have the little tête-à-tête's and discussions together, and you think, innocently, "Isn't it nice that my husband has so much in common with my best friend?"

BILL: And we've even had people tell us, "I thought it was so wonderful that he was spending this time with my best friend. I thought they were probably planning my birthday party."

(laughter)

COLIN: Oh dear.

BILL: It was a little different than what she thought.

COLIN: Is it more common . . . I don't know if it breaks down this way or not, for a male or a female to have an affair with the spouse's best friend?

BILL: Actually, based on over three thousand and two hundred couples we've seen, it's about equal.

CAROLYN: . . . Yes, it could happen in either direction. What happens is that the spouse who has been hurt by this is absolutely devastated. Because the people they most trusted, the people that they felt they could share all their emotions and vulnerabilities with, have betrayed them.

COLIN: Yes, the person . . . must feel terribly isolated.

BILL: Oh, it's a terrific hurt.

CAROLYN: Yes, yes.

BILL: You see, if your partner goes outside your relationship with someone else, at least you have a friend that can give you support. But now your partner's gone out with your best friend. Who do you turn to? All your best support systems are gone also.

COLIN: Is the best friend, the one with whom the partner has the affair – is that person often involved in a relationship as well?

CAROLYN: Yes.

BILL: . . . Usually they are married as well. So, you see, the pain now involves four people. And ironically, the new relationship, hardly ever works out, in fact, statistically, they almost all fall apart.

CAROLYN: Uh huhhh.

BILL: So what happens now, is that you have four people who are hurt. Initially, it was two people, but eventually you have four people in a lot of pain.

COLIN: When the aggrieved spouse finds out, can the relationship with her husband or his wife be salvaged?

BILL: Yes.

CAROLYN: Yes, it can, Colin. It is absolutely amazing to us, the amount of commitment that is often in the relationship. Sometimes, even though the spouse has gone outside the relationship with the best friend, if both members of the relationship want to stay in the relationship and feel that it can go on, then the relationship can be salvaged, but they really need to have professional help.

BILL: It is absolutely essential that the best friend is put aside. Maybe we can have a look at Jerry and Ann, who illustrate that they realize some big mistakes have been made, and they want to now get together and salvage their relationship.Can we meet Jerry and Ann?

COLIN: Certainly.

CAROLYN: Okay, so Jerry's actually gone outside their relationship with Ann's best friend . . .

JERRY: "Ann, I know I'm supposed to end the affair, but couldn't we just sort of remain best friends with her?"

ANN: "I find that too painful. I can't handle that."

JERRY: "But couldn't we remain friends with her and her husband, and you know, couldn't we go out and at least double date together once in a while?"

ANN: "I just can't handle that."

BILL: Do you notice what's happening Colin?

COLIN: Yes.

BILL: . . . What's happening here is that his partner, Ann, is in a lot of pain, but Jerry still wants to hold on to some old ties.

CAROLYN: . . . What occurs is . . . he feels a tremendous amount of guilt, because he's gone outside the relationship, and he's also taken away her best friend. So he sort of pushes her into having a liaison again with the best friend, feeling that this may help her ease some of the pain, and she says it's too painful. An even more sinister reason may be that he feels if he has to break off this affair, maybe he will still be able to see the friend if they go out on a double date together. And we call this the double date from hell.

(laughter)

CAROLYN: There's nothing worse, because the wife then is continually imagining what it was like for her husband to be with her best friend. It's one of the most painful experiences she will ever have.

COLIN: Well, I can't imagine such a date, because the best friend was also involved in the relationship.

BILL: Exactly. Now, it's hard for us to imagine that this could occur with anybody who is in a committed relationship, but we see this happening repeatedly. The attitude of the person who's gone outside the relationship – is that they just don't want to break it off completely; they still want to hang on a little bit . . .

CAROLYN: . . . And they can't . . .

BILL: No. The key to salvaging of this relationship is that they must break it off – this is no longer a best friend . . .

CAROLYN: . . . Exactly. These are not people you want to be spending time with. If it's going to be fun time, you want to have some other friends you can start going out with. Another thing, too, Colin, is that there are certain signs that may point to trouble in the relationship, that may indicate the potential of one of them having a relationship with somebody else. One indicator is if a marital partner feels he or she can no longer talk to the spouse. They feel a lot of tension whenever they share emotions and feelings. They sense the spouse feels very bored or that they're just wasting their time.

BILL: Sometimes they stop eating together at mealtimes.

CAROLYN: That's a big one . . . they stop having supper together.

BILL: Right.

CAROLYN: One of them will work very long hours in the evening and grab a quick bite on the way home. They stop having mealtimes together and when they do eat together it is no longer enjoyable.

BILL: Another thing that we hear is that they begin to grab on to the edge of their own side of the bed at night. Sometimes they don't even sleep together.

CAROLYN: . . . Or they may be sleeping together, but the dog's sleeping between them.

(laughter)

BILL: Right.

COLIN: Early warning signs, coupled with your spouse showing a lot of interest in your best friend may be something to watch out for.

BILL: . . . That's right. The first signs we mentioned just now are fairly general. They could be indicators for any relationship in trouble, but what you've noted are the little signs that indicate that maybe it's the friend who really is the main factor here.

CAROLYN: Right. The friend begins to say, "You're so lucky to have your husband. He understands me so much better than my husband does."

BILL: And your friend wants to find out just a little bit more about your relationship.

CAROLYN: Yes!

BILL: These are little warning signs that should go on in your head, they show that maybe some caution is needed.

COLIN: . . . It must be a terribly sensitive subject to broach though, with your husband or your best friend.

CAROLYN: Yes, sometimes when people are suspicious, they use devious means to find out what may be happening. They find out that the friend is going up to the lake at the same time that the husband is, which would seem quite innocent, because they both have cottages at the lake. But there seem to be little meetings that you would ordinarily not have been suspicious about, but now there seem to be more frequent late visits . . .

BILL: Your friend phones to talk to you, and in the meantime, your husband speaks to her for quite a long time before he hands over the phone.

CAROLYN: Yes, and you think, isn't that nice and friendly.

(laughter)

CAROLYN: But suddenly you realize there is just too much closeness between them. They've crossed the line.

BILL: Exactly. So the hurt is there. This is the ultimate betrayal, Colin.

CAROLYN: Right.

BILL: The hurt – or the fact that the betrayal has occurred, or the affair has occurred – can never be erased, but the pain, in time, can disappear.

CAROLYN: Yes Colin, with appropriate therapy Ann and Jerry can rebuild their relationship. But they generally cannot do it on their own. They need professional help to learn how to regain their trust in each other.

COLIN: Okay, Bill, Carolyn, thanks very much.

CAROLYN: Good, thank you, Colin.

BILL: Thank you, Colin.

QUOTES FROM COUPLES

We have a problem in our marriage,
I could tell you her name!

You're such a nice woman,
I can't understand why I'm so unhappy married to you.

LOVE AT THE OFFICE

COLIN GREWAR: We spend a lot of time at work, so we get to know the people we work with pretty well. For some co-workers, that friendship grows into, well, into something more romantic, into a relationship. It could be wonderful, but there are risks. Joining me now to talk about love at the office are Dr. Bill and Carolyn Chernenkoff, co-therapists in marital and sexual counselling in Saskatoon. Hello, Bill, Carolyn.

CAROLYN: Hello, Colin.

BILL: Hi, Colin.

COLIN: You know, I guess it's natural that people would develop attractions to other people at their work place.

BILL: Yes!

CAROLYN: Oh, is it ever, Colin. Cupid may be beckoning in the corridors of the company.

(laughter)

BILL: Exactly.

CAROLYN: It's very common, because it is their natural community, especially if it's a large company or corporation. At times you get to know the people that you're working with very well.

BILL: It's basically the natural dating service, isn't it. You know the people and you see them in action. It's a dating game.

CAROLYN: Right, and it's a safe situation. You know all the people that you're with. You can see: Are they capable? Are they responsible? How do they react to other people? How do they handle crises? Do they have temper tantrums? Do they have a sense of humor? What you're looking at is, you have a good proximity to the game, you can watch the players, and you know all the numbers on the uniforms.

COLIN: You get to see all sides of this person.

CAROLYN: Do you ever.

COLIN: The good and maybe the bad.

CAROLYN: Yes.

COLIN: Of course, there are other dynamics in a work environment that may not be there in a dating environment. I would imagine that would especially be the case if the person you're attracted to is your boss.

CAROLYN: Oh, yes.

BILL: Now that's where we would recommend, that it should be a horizontal liaison, no pun intended *(laughter)*, rather than a vertical liaison. Vertical liaisons, meaning an employee/boss supervisor relationship, do not usually work out. Somebody's going to be hurt, probably both people.

CAROLYN: That's a prescription for disaster. It does not work. It should be somebody who is on equal terms with you; somebody that you do not have to report to, or who has no control over whether or not you advance in the company. Even horizontal liaisons can be a little bit touchy. It does begin to change the dynamics in the office setting when you have a romantic liaison with a co-worker.

COLIN: Yes, it could be one of the risks. We talked about some of the good things. You get a really good look at this person, but what are some of the other risks involved, when you're looking for love at the office?

BILL: Well, one of the risks is that plunging productivity can occur. What happens is that gossip around the water cooler begins to overpower what's happening at the office. The energy of the other employees begins to go into talking about the liaison going on, rather than what they're supposed to be doing at work.

CAROLYN: You may be the object of that gossip. There may be all sorts of stories going around. People may react to you differently, may ask you little questions, give little digs, a little teasing. It may take away from the energy that you usually put into your job.

BILL: Another aspect is the fishbowl world of the office. It's almost impossible to keep any secrets from anyone in the office.

CAROLYN: That's right. There's not much confidentiality. Everybody knows everybody else's business. It's like a small community because people tell stories all the time. You may be a part of that breaking of confidentiality as well.

COLIN: And I guess you have to look ahead. I'm just imagining, suppose you start off really well with this person, then you have an argument, a split, who knows. All of a sudden your work environment is pretty uncomfortable.

BILL: That's right. There certainly are risks involved with this. What could be a blossoming romance could become a fatal distraction. "What if this relationship doesn't work out? What if ends? What disaster will occur?"

CAROLYN: What happens with outside the office relationships, Colin, is that if you have a relationship that breaks up, you can continue going to your workplace. You don't have to deal with that person every day. But if you break up a relationship with a co-worker, and then you have to continue seeing them on a day-to-day basis at the office, it can be a very uncomfortable situation.

BILL: So, you'll have to think, not only is there love at the office, but there can be hate at the office as well.

CAROLYN: Yes, the love can turn to hate.

BILL: We have Stewart and Heather with us who can illustrate just what's happening in their situation.

CAROLYN: Stewart and Heather have been in a relationship, and it's not working out well for them at all. This is a private moment away from the office. Heather says to Stewart . . .

HEATHER: "I no longer want to be in this relationship. This is not working well. I'll continue to see you at work, but the relationship is over."

STEWART: "You'll live to regret this, Heather. I'll make your life miserable."

CAROLYN: Oooh!

BILL: Oooh! And he does. The miserableness can be in the form of harassment, actual physical or verbal harassment, or sometimes it can be spreading personal and confidential information about the other person. Sometimes the personal and confidential information is false.

CAROLYN: And it becomes very uncomfortable.

COLIN: . . . You probably go to work dreading running into him or her in the elevator or at the photocopy machine.

CAROLYN: Exactly, Colin. You spend your time hiding behind your desk. You don't want to meet him beside the coffee machine, you can't even look him in the face. You wonder how much information the other employees at the company know. It's really uncomfortable. Those are some of the consequences. Those are the things that you have to look at.

COLIN: So, what advice do you have for people who find themselves attracted to someone at work, and who may be thinking of striking up a relationship of some kind?

BILL: Good question. First of all, it's really important to look at – "What if this doesn't work out? Will I be able to keep on working with this person, in this environment, if the relationship ends?"

That's probably the most crucial consideration.

CAROLYN: Yes, and the next one is that, definitely . . . married people are off limits. That is a destructive situation for each person involved, so it's definitely taboo.

BILL: And it shouldn't be used as a way of getting ahead. If it's a boss\employee relationship, that's exploitation. In other words, if the employee is trying to get ahead of everybody else by having a relationship with the boss, that's definitely a disaster plan.

CAROLYN: And then if it's an employee\employer situation and the employer is starting the relationship because the other person is an employee then that is a power and control trip, so that's not good.

BILL: Another concern is to be sure to keep the relationship private. There should be no personal interaction going on between the two people in the office.

CAROLYN: Or even the parking lot.

BILL: Personal contact should be kept for private moments.

CAROLYN: You also have to continue to put a lot of energy into your job. People will be watching to see if it's affecting your productivity. You don't know, this relationship may not last as long as your job does. You don't want to jeopardize your job. That's the most important thing.

BILL: And so, Colin, if the office doesn't say it's taboo, and if both people are unattached. . .

CAROLYN: And if it's not with your boss, then certainly this may be the potential for a very natural setting to develop into a good relationship.

BILL: And sometimes the benefits of that can be better than a dental plan.

CAROLYN: Yes, exactly.

BILL: And it is possible to find love and success under one cosy, corporate roof.

CAROLYN: If you play by the rules.

(laugher)

COLIN: Okay. Bill, Carolyn, thanks very much.

CAROLYN: Good, thank you, Colin.

BILL: Thanks, Colin.

QUOTES FROM COUPLES

My penis has become smaller since my wife divorced me.

It's like he is behind a glass wall. I can see him,
but there is no sound. It's like living with a vacuum.

TRIGGER POINTS IN A RELATIONSHIP

COLIN GREWAR: In every relationship, no matter how perfect, there are little things that bother each partner about the other. If those little things grow into major confrontations or conflicts, and they can, problems arise. Dr. Bill and Carolyn Chernenkoff are co-therapists in marital and sexual counselling in Saskatoon. They join me now to talk about trigger points. Hello, Bill, Carolyn.

CAROLYN: Hi, Colin.

BILL: Hi, good afternoon, Colin.

COLIN: What types of trigger points are we talking about here?

CAROLYN: We hear almost everything, Colin. The common ones that we hear about are money management, relatives . . . housework is also a big one . . .

BILL: . . . That is a big one . . .

CAROLYN: . . . And job pressures, scheduling, . . . things like that.

BILL: But it can be almost anything. It can get right down to the noise that one partner makes when eating . . .

(laughter)

BILL: . . . We kid you not, we've heard it all.

CAROLYN: It's really interesting, Colin, when we're counselling couples, usually, after the third or fourth session, we say to them, "Tomorrow we'd like you to bring us a trigger point. This is an area that you know – if this topic is brought up – it's going to end in a confrontation." As soon as we say trigger point, there's a big smile from the couple across the table, because they know what it is. It's the area that's left on the back burner, and it sort of stews and festers. It can be very disruptive in the relationship.

BILL: Most couples have about three or four that permeate their life at any particular time . . .

CAROLYN: . . . Yes . . .

BILL: . . . And the dilemma, or the destructive effect that it causes, just never gets resolved.

CAROLYN: No.

BILL: It just keeps repeating itself over and over and over. Sometimes there's silence for hours or sometimes days or weeks. After a confrontation about this topic, they may not talk to each other for weeks.

COLIN: Well . . . don't they realize that it's the little things that are causing this sort of chilliness toward each other. Surely people can understand that it's just a little thing – that it can be resolved.

BILL: Well, very often they know – and sometimes they even say, "We have arguments, or we have silent times over the stupidest things."

CAROLYN: Yes.

BILL: But they sometimes don't know how to get out of the situation or what to do with it.

CAROLYN: And sometimes also, Colin, it's a power struggle . . . "My way is the only way."

(laughter)

CAROLYN: And they don't know how to negotiate their differences gracefully, with each saving face. To give in, as they see themselves doing, would mean they're the loser.

BILL: Exactly. We recently had just such a couple. May we call them Peter and Joan?

COLIN: Sure.

BILL: They have a common trigger point which is, "When it is time to leave a social gathering, or party?"

CAROLYN: . . . Yes . . .

BILL: . . . That's a very common thing . . .

CAROLYN: . . . This is something that many couples do, weekly or monthly. They say, "Every time we go out, the same thing happens." And it really creates distress in the relationship.

BILL: So here is Peter approaching Joan, in the middle of a group of people, and everybody hears this conversation. He says . . .

PETER: "Okay Joan, time to go now, let's go, right now."

JOAN: "Who made you boss and forgot to tell me?"

PETER: "Well, come on, come on, come on, let's get in the car right now."

JOAN: "I'm staying."

PETER: "All right. Stay!"

JOAN: "I will."

(laughter)

CAROLYN: You noticed the power struggle there?

COLIN: And this happens at every party they go to?

CAROLYN: Oh, yes, every party. In fact, it even starts before they get to the party. He says . . .

PETER: "Okay, we're leaving the party in an hour and a half. Now, you be sure to understand this. We're only staying for an hour and a half."

JOAN: "We're not going to stay more than an hour and a half?"

PETER: "No."

JOAN: "Well, what's the sense of even going. I might as well just stay home."

(laughter)

BILL: Exactly, it begins to permeate their lives. Then, of course, when Joan does go with Peter, when they get home, there's a lot of tension, and it's pretty much silent all the way home.

CAROLYN: And the silence may last until the next morning.

BILL: That's right.

COLIN: Or longer, I guess . . .

CAROLYN: . . . Yes, or longer . . . they may get on to another topic the next morning, but what happens in this situation is that when she hears his demand, "We're going," she very often feels rebellious. She thinks, "I'll do what I want to. I'll dig in my heels and I'll show you, I'm not going." So, what they have to look at – in most scenarios, is this: What is the situation; how does it affect them; what options do they see to solve the problem?

BILL: So, if we take the same scenario, Peter needs to look at his attitude – why does he always demand to go home so early? What are his feelings? Well, the reason probably is that he's got to get to work the next morning, or he may not be having a good time. We don't know that at this stage. But it may be . . . that he's got an obligation for the next morning. So Peter and Joan learn that it can be approached a little differently. The next time they're in a situation like this and he has a chance to talk to her away from everybody else, so that everybody is not embarrassed . . . he says something like this . . .

PETER: "Joan, I've had a good time, but I really have to go. I've got to get up early tomorrow morning, and I really have to go."

JOAN: "I can understand that. I'd like to stay for another fifteen minutes. I'd like to just thank our hosts, and then I'll be ready to go."

PETER: "Okay, actually, I'd like to thank them as well."

JOAN: "Okay."

PETER: "That'd be terrific. I've had a good time, but I really have to go."

CAROLYN: Okay, they are having some negotiation here. She knows that he's really tired and he has to get up early. Maybe she'd like to stay a little bit longer, but she knows there are trade offs and she knows this is one she can be flexible on. They've reached an agreement, and both have saved face.

BILL: And he's been a little bit more flexible. Actually, he's indicated that he hasn't had a bad time. As well, you see that he's not demanding, and she knows why he has to get home, because he does have to go to work the next day.

CAROLYN: Right.

COLIN: So in every trigger point case, it involves a negotiation particular to whatever that trigger point may be, whether it's money or relatives or even, as you mentioned, Carolyn, the noise he makes when he eats.

(laughter)

CAROLYN: Actually, Bill said that and it really does happen. To give you an example of negotiating or signalling, one couple that we saw – they described it to us very well – said, "You know, it's as if the car ahead of you turns and it doesn't signal, and you say under your breath, 'Well, thank you very much for not telling me what you were going to do.'" If you indicate what you're feeling, "I'm tired, I want to go home, this is how I feel," it's like making the signals before you make the turn, and then the traffic runs more smoothly.

BILL: So Peter gives a little signal as to why he wants to go home . . . first by identifying what his feelings are and then indicating what his needs are. That way Joan knows which direction the car is turning.

COLIN: It's as simple as that, and it can make for a much happier ride home.

(laughter)

COLIN: Okay, Bill, Carolyn, thank you very much.

BILL: Thank you.

CAROLYN: Good, thanks, Colin.

QUOTES FROM COUPLES

If our house was on fire, I would not give my husband the satisfaction of phoning him to let him know.

Nobody does the housework in our house – it looks like a pack of wild dogs have been running around loose inside.

She has multiple orgasms – one year she had two.

Sex & Humor

COLIN GREWAR: Sex is important to any long-lasting relationship, but that doesn't mean it has to be serious business. On the contrary, you should have a few laughs in the bedroom. That's what Dr. Bill and Carolyn Chernenkoff say. Bill and Carolyn are co-therapists in marital and sexual counselling in Saskatoon, and they join me now to talk about Sex and Humor. Hello, Carolyn, Bill.

CAROLYN: Hello.

BILL: Hi, Colin.

COLIN: So, why is humor an important ingredient for good sex?

CAROLYN: Well usually, Colin, if the couple is having fun together, if they can let down their guard and enjoy each other's company and have a good laugh, it usually leads to good sex as well. Sex can be the most intimate form of communication. It's a means of reproduction, but it's also supposed to be fun.

BILL: And you know, we learn about fun right from the beginning, when we are young, from our parents. What do they do with us? They tickle us, they sing rhymes to us. They lift us up over their shoulders, and what do we do? We laugh and giggle, we love it.

CAROLYN: Yes.

BILL: And we often lose that ability to have fun. I like what you said at the beginning, you said it becomes so serious sometimes.

COLIN: Well, I guess it does. You know, Carolyn and Bill, every two weeks you come on the show, and we talk about the sexual problems that people have. There's lots of room for things to go wrong, a lot of disappointments. The earth may not move every time.

CAROLYN: Yes, yes.

COLIN: I guess that is when the sense of humor becomes most important.

CAROLYN: Exactly Colin . . . We find couples who, if things don't work out . . . they can laugh about it and joke around about it, and not get too serious . . . When that happens, it's much more likely that they won't get into the dysfunction and sexual distress.

BILL: Exactly.

CAROLYN: Very often we have this feeling that sex is supposed to be so serious. I know when we first started teaching, we thought sex was . . . we had to talk about it with such seriousness. But actually, even in the role playings that we use, we put in some humor, and some of them are really corny. But it breaks the tension. Sometimes when you use a little bit of humor, it's easier to laugh at things, and you feel a little bit more relaxed.

BILL: It just makes everybody feel more comfortable.

CAROLYN: Yes.

BILL: At least it makes us feel comfortable. *(laughter)*

COLIN: What do you mean by humor, exactly, in the context of sex?

BILL: Well, we don't mean being a standup comic on the David Letterman show, or wearing a gorilla or clown suit. Unless that's your thing, of course.

CAROLYN: Yes, and I guess what we mean is being able to laugh at your mistakes and your partner's mistakes. You should be able to be very vulnerable. Suppose you're in an intimate situation, and the kids start banging at the bedroom door and the telephone rings . . . if a person makes it into a catastrophe and says, "This is terrible. Why does it always happen to us?" It doesn't leave a very positive feeling. They don't look at the humorous side of things.

BILL: They feel sort of bitter and unsettled. Instead, if they can laugh at it, "Well, next time it'll work out better," then it neutralizes the stress and things will more likely work out better!

COLIN: Of course, when you start joking around in any situation, Carolyn, you often risk hurting someone's feelings.

CAROLYN: How true.

BILL: Actually . . . let's meet Irma and Stan? They use humor, but it is in a subtle putdown form . . . quite destructive.

COLIN: Irma and Stan?

BILL: Yes.

CAROLYN: Colin, what we commonly see is that couples very often will get into this situation. Irma says to Stan . . .

IRMA: "You know, Ann's husband is much worse than you are. He watches television all day long."

STAN: "And I betcha she needs a much bigger truck to go shopping than you do."

IRMA: "What do you mean by that?"

STAN: "Ah, just kidding."

(laughter)

BILL: So, you'll notice there's sort of a twisted humor there. It is humor, but it's at the expense of the other person.

CAROLYN: Yes, and very often when we see couples for counselling, either one or both are making jabs at the other person all the time. They will say, "Well, I was just kidding, it was really funny," But the other person will say, "It was very hurtful." They build up hurts as the day progresses, and the other individual develops a lot of resentment.

COLIN: Yes, you do see that with a lot of couples, where one partner is always putting down the other, maybe even in a group setting that everyone else finds funny. But you know, you don't realize how much it may be hurting the one who's the brunt of the jokes.

CAROLYN: Yes, the one who is the brunt may laugh at it, and think it's easy just to put up with it, but it builds a lot of hurt inside. That hurt sits and festers and it eventually becomes anger.

BILL: Now suppose Irma and Stan had a humor class.

CAROLYN: Yes, a one-hour humor class, and they've learned that in order to have some fun, it's more healthy to laugh at themselves instead of at their partners.

BILL: Suppose they've gone to a wonderful gourmet restaurant, and they've just had a fantastic meal. As they're leaving the restaurant, Irma says,

IRMA: "I feel so full, I am absolutely stuffed. I feel like a Sumo wrestler. I think my stomach is sticking out further than my breasts."

STAN: "I thought it was just me. I had to let my belt out a notch. I can't walk."

IRMA: "Well, let's roll down the street together."

STAN: "I think I'll have to."

CAROLYN: So, what you have, Colin, is a partner in crime, because this woman is being incredibly vulnerable to her partner.

BILL: And so is he. They're just goofing together, basically, and just having a good time, but not at the other person's expense. They're making fun of themselves, not each other. They've enjoyed the experience together.

CAROLYN: Yes, and when you can laugh with the other, rather than at the other, it also makes that person feel more at ease. They don't have to have their guard up, because you're putting yourself down rather than putting down the other person.

COLIN: Yes, and in the context of sex, I guess, it's, important to lighten up a little bit when things don't always go the way they're supposed to go.

CAROLYN: Yes, when your partner crawls into bed with his black socks on. *(laughter)* It's easy to laugh at the situation rather than get into a pout or a snit.

BILL: Exactly, the black socks on a naked body may be the most unsexy thing, but yet they can laugh at it, AND . . . having a good laugh together is like a caress. It makes you feel all warm inside. Basically what it says is, "I like being with you."

CAROLYN: "And I feel comfortable with you."

BILL: And you know, a couple that giggles together . . . if you giggle with somebody that you really adore, it can be absolutely refreshing. . . . It may be one of the most satisfying things that a couple can do together.

CAROLYN: Yes, even better than good sex sometimes, and if you have a good laugh together, the sex may get better.

COLIN: Okay, Bill, Carolyn, thanks very much.

CAROLYN: Okay, thanks, Colin.

BILL: A pleasure.

QUOTES FROM COUPLES

When my partner and I are making love,
we look like two beached whales.

When I was able to get an erection, my wife stood up at the
side of the bed and sang, "Happy days are here again."

PUTTING ROMANCE BACK INTO RELATIONSHIPS

COLIN GREWAR: Valentine's Day is a day for love and romance. That makes it a pretty happy day for many couples, but for many more it can be a sad and uncomfortable day. All this talk of flowers, chocolates, love and kisses has a very empty ring to it if the romance has gone out of your relationship. Instead of enjoying this day of hearts, perhaps you're trying to figure out just where you and your partner went wrong. Well, it may not be too late to change things. Joining me now to talk about keeping romance alive are Dr. Bill & Carolyn Chernenkoff, co-therapists in marital and sexual counselling, in Saskatoon. Hello, Carolyn, Bill.

CAROLYN: Hello, Colin

BILL: Hi, Colin, Good Afternoon.

COLIN: And Happy Valentine's Day.

CAROLYN & BILL: Thank you and the same to you.

COLIN: I guess Valentine's Day can be a day of rather sad realization for many people involved in relationships.

BILL: Yes, actually that's true. Sometimes the spark that they used to have begins to disappear.

CAROLYN: And there may be some emptiness in the relationship.

BILL: We have a scenario with Christine and John. We'd like to paint a picture of what happened on their Valentine's Day.

CAROLYN: It's Valentine's Day, it's 10:00 o'clock in the evening, and Christine is propped up in bed, working on a presentation for the next morning.

BILL: John slides into bed beside her. He dims the light to a sensual glow, and places an elegantly wrapped gift on her lap. He whispers into her ear . . .

JOHN: "You know, Christine, we've been under a lot of stress lately. Maybe this will help."

CAROLYN: Christine opens the parcel and finds a video, some colorful condoms and some body lotion.

BILL: As John touches her gently, their embrace is suddenly broken by a cry from the baby monitor on the bedroom wall.

CAROLYN: And they both stiffen, but not from lust, as the cries break out into a constant wail. After half an hour of trying to get the baby back to sleep, they have both lost all desire.

BILL: This scenario is probably replayed in many homes today.

(laughter)

COLIN: Now that's a situation where, clearly, I guess, family responsibilities lead to a reduced interest in romance or reduced opportunities for it.

BILL: You know, Colin, that's probably the most common reason . . . because family responsibilities and work schedules interfere with the romance in the couple's relationship.

CAROLYN: Sometimes, when you have all these pressures, making time for love is somewhere below getting time to do the breakfast dishes.

(laughter)

BILL: And exhaustion is usually not a turn on!

CAROLYN: No, it's way down on the list.

COLIN: You know, in the '90s when both partners in a relationship are usually working, there must be all sorts of extra stresses.

CAROLYN: Yes! Often what a woman is doing now, Colin, is working full time and she has a family. She has her job as a parent, her job as a homemaker and also her professional role. She's suffering from time and work overload, having too many things to do in too short a time.

BILL: And the working parents with young children are probably the most vulnerable to losing their sense of romance. In the first part of the marriage, when the couple are still in the romantic phase, they usually turn inward towards each other, the rest of the world is outside. But, when the pressures of work and children begin to coincide, then they're most at risk of losing the romance.

CAROLYN: A lot of couples that we see are in that stage. They're almost like roommates. They're living individual lives, but they're under one roof. They're almost on parallel lines that don't intersect at all. There's no emotional closeness or intimacy.

COLIN: So, what can a couple do to rekindle that flame?

BILL: Well, Colin, that's really important. What they need to do is to talk about it. That's probably the ingredient most lacking. They stop holding each other, stop hugging each other, stop touching each other, and they stop talking to each other as well.

CAROLYN: One of the most common things that we hear from females is that she thinks that his desire is similar to what it was when they were first married, which may have been ten or fifteen years ago. When they were first together, she thought that whenever she touched him, he would immediately want sex and make a fifty-yard dash to the bedroom.

(laughter)

BILL: And usually he did. He was younger and more virile at that stage, and it always seemed like it was going to end up in intercourse, at least that's the message she got. But, as they've been

married, his feelings and needs change. He may not want intercourse each time. He just wants more intimacy now, but the problem is that she doesn't know that.

CAROLYN: . . . She doesn't know that, yet that's what her needs
are as well. But they've never talked about it. They need to get it
out in the open and find out where they're at. They need to find
out what each other's needs really are.

COLIN: And by intimacy you're referring to something other than
just sex.

BILL: Absolutely!

CAROLYN: The closeness, the affection, just during the day, that
is what brings out the romance. It makes you feel like you're really
wanted in this relationship, that you're cared for and important.

BILL: Intimacy is much more than just sex. The closeness and
companionship are important. We compare it to an accordion – it
comes together, goes apart, comes together, but always there's a
link that binds the couple together. That link brings them back.
They want to be linked together, because the achievements, their
accomplishments that they share bring them approval and accep-
tance from each other.

CAROLYN: Actually, when they're with their partners, that's
when they feel accepted, really feel good. They get emotional support from each other.

COLIN: As far as the sexual thing goes though, Bill and Carolyn, a
lot of couples look in men's and women's magazines, and read that
they should be doing it a certain number of times a month. If
they're not, they may think they're not in a healthy marriage.
Should people be intimidated, threatened, by these statistics?

BILL: Oh, that's a good question, Colin.

CAROLYN: No, a lot of that is somebody's fantasy. Sometimes
those questionnaires are not filled out accurately. Whatever is

meeting the couple's needs should be satisfying and enjoyable for them, rather than feeling they need to match up to something.

BILL: Whether it's 2.3 times per week or 2.3 times per month, it really doesn't matter. It's according to what the couple's needs are. It's interesting though, Colin, that, at this stage, the couple's main difficulty is usually finding the time and energy for sex, that's more of a problem for them.

CAROLYN: It's almost like when people are going to exercise. It's trying to get the energy to get into it. But once they get into it, both members of the relationship say, "Gosh, I wouldn't have missed that for the world. I really had a good time. How come it took so long for me to make time for it."

COLIN: Yes, what you're saying, Bill and Carolyn, is that it's easy to fall out of romance; you have to work at it to get it back.

CAROLYN: It does take effort, Colin, and it often comes to a situation where it almost needs to be scheduled, like anything else that's really important. When you have a busy life, you have to make time for your sex life too.

BILL: You know, if we make an appointment to take our car in for servicing, usually we don't miss it. Why? Because it's important for the maintenance of the car. Well, a relationship is probably even more important than a car. It needs scheduling and time as well. It needs priority. The couple needs to make a "couple time" appointment, and stick with it. That's really important.

COLIN: Really, like saying on a Thursday morning, tomorrow night, this is what we're going to do?

BILL: Absolutely!

CAROLYN: Exactly. It's not time set aside specifically for intercourse, but just to have time to be together. Out of that may spring some desire and interest, but you need to, first of all, have that time with your partner.

BILL: Nowadays, couples who are busy working, career people, it's really important for them to schedule that time together.

COLIN: Hmmm. . . schedule it, if you go to this trouble – if you make the effort, certainly there are rewards.

BILL: Oh, yes!

CAROLYN: Yes! And I guess the good news is this, Colin, actually John and Christine did have an opportunity to try out John's Valentine's surprise.

COLIN: *(laughter)* Oh they did?

BILL: Yes, they did. They checked into a motel on Sunday, and the surprise was wonderful. It was very enjoyable for them.

CAROLYN: They found a baby sitter for the baby.

BILL: That's the key. Scheduling the time was crucial.

CAROLYN: Yes. Actually, there are some very positive benefits, Colin, to lovemaking. One of them is that lovemaking can definitely decrease the windchill factor by 50 percent. And as you noted, Valentine's day is warmer.

(laughter)

COLIN: Yes.

BILL: And, actually, you don't need to reserve a court for it.

(laughter)

CAROLYN: No, that's true. You can turn a bad day into a really good night.

COLIN: Bill, Carolyn, thank you very much.

CAROLYN: Thank you, Colin.

BILL: Thank you very much, Colin.

WHAT MAKES SUCCESSFUL RELATIONSHIPS?

COLIN GREWAR: We hear a lot about relationships that aren't working. About people breaking up, getting divorced or separating. Considering the pressures of living in the '90s, I guess we shouldn't really be surprised at that. Living with someone isn't always easy. The odds are stacked against you finding the person you can spend the rest of your life with, but it can happen, and it does happen, a lot. What makes a successful relationship? That's what Dr. Bill and Carolyn Chernenkoff are going to talk about today. Bill and Carolyn are co-therapists in marital and sexual counselling in Saskatoon. Hello, Bill, Carolyn.

CAROLYN: Hi, Colin.

BILL: Good afternoon, Colin.

COLIN: What is the first thing you notice about couples that have a relationship that is working?

BILL: Oh, they're happy.

(laughter)

CAROLYN: Yes, Colin. When you're in a good relationship, you feel good, and when you're in a bad relationship, you feel bad. Actually, when the relationship is working, it gives you a lot of energy. You just feel good about life in general.

BILL: And you know, in over twenty years, we've seen over three thousand, two hundred couples. We found there was a common thread through all of the really good solid relationships. They all had symptoms of good love.

COLIN: Symptoms of good love?

(laughter)

CAROLYN: Yes.

COLIN: And what's the first symptom?

CAROLYN: Well, the first one, Colin, is that they're very good friends. They do have other close friends, but their partner is the person that they feel they can share emotions and vulnerabilities with. And these shared confidences are never going to be used against them. They won't be taken advantage of.

BILL: Actually, Colin, they put their relatives and even their best friend secondary to their partner. Their partner is way ahead.

CAROLYN: Yes.

BILL: They laugh together. They have a great time together. Basically, what they're saying is, "I feel that you accept me as I am, even if I'm silly or goofy sometimes."

(laughter)

COLIN: I have a lot of good friends, though, Bill and Carolyn, that I don't think I'd want to be married to. There's something more there. Friendship is clearly an important part, but what's there in addition to that? More than being good friends?

BILL: That's very observant. That extra ingredient is the commitment in the relationship.

CAROLYN: Yes, and the commitment, Colin, is that "I promise to be with you because I want to be, not because I have to be." This is the person I want to be with. There is a feeling that they put a tremendous amount of energy into the relationship. The idea of going outside of the relationship with another person is totally out of the question.

BILL: "It's just simply good to be with you," is the feeling of commitment.

COLIN: Now, Carolyn and Bill, I know one of your favorite slogans is *SEX is a thirteen-letter word*. You quizzed me about this some months ago, and now I know what the word is, it's **COMMUNICATION**.

CAROLYN: You've got it!

COLIN: What's happening in that regard, when a relationship is working well?

BILL: Well, this is when there are good messages being sent about sharing; identifying their feelings and emotions. And there's another ingredient that we haven't really talked about.

CAROLYN: What that is, Colin, is that there needs to be both a sender and a receiver. There has to be a listener. It is like this – if you have a ship in the middle of the ocean frantically sending out S.O.S. signals, and nobody picking up the signals, that ship is going to sink.

BILL: We've brought Sharon and Kevin with us to illustrate what happened when no receiver was tuned in. May we share that with you?

COLIN: Yes.

BILL: Well, here's Kevin. He's home from work, and he's sitting in the living room. He's got a newspaper in one hand and a remote control for the T.V. set in the other hand. Sharon is in the kitchen and says . . .

SHARON: "I had a rotten day at work. Everything went wrong. One of the other staff didn't show up, and I had their job to do plus my job to do, and I ran out of gas on the way home, and I don't have any idea what to have for supper."

KEVIN: Uh huhhh!

SHARON: "Can you play back to me what I just said; what's your understanding of what I just said?"

KEVIN: "What? Oh! One of the staff at work had some rotten gas?"

SHARON: "No!"

(laughter)

BILL: So, he's not picked up on this message at all.

CAROLYN: She's sending out really good messages, but they're not being picked up. She needs to get his attention. She may need to go into the room he's in. She may have to turn off the T.V., nicely, and touch his hand.

BILL: And get eye contact with him. Then she says . . .

SHARON: "I need to share this with you. This is really important. I had a rotten day at work. Everything went wrong. I ran out of gas on the way home, and I don't have any idea what to have for supper. That's sort of it."

KEVIN: "I had a pretty good day, actually. Things really went well, I sort of rested up a little bit, so I'll offer to get supper. It will take about fifteen minutes. Then I can sit down with you when I have dinner together. I'll get it ready."

SHARON: "I just need to relax. I really appreciate your understanding."

BILL: The message got through because the receiver received it.

COLIN: It also got through because the sender made an effort to send it in a nice way.

CAROLYN: Yes, exactly. It's not threatening, and it's not accusatory. What they did was, when they began to see a breakdown in communication, they resolved it immediately, rather than letting it build and eventually result in a conflict.

BILL: That's the key for couples who are successful in their relationship. Sharon didn't attack Kevin for not listening. She made an effort to modify the interaction without it being threatening to Kevin.

COLIN: Now, Bill and Carolyn, what about when things aren't rosy? Bad things happen in life, crises come up and often they are the true test of a relationship. What happens between two people, in a good relationship, when a crisis occurs?

CAROLYN: Well, Colin, they're emotionally supportive of each other. If you don't get the promotion at work, or if you lose your job, you know your partner is going to give you emotional support. He or she is not going to blame you; he's going to make you feel that it's going to be okay.

BILL: And these are the partners who bring out . . . accentuate the positive . . . What they are really saying is, "Your feelings are important to me, and when you feel good, that's when I feel good. I want to contribute to your feeling good." That's the support . . . that is what is constantly going on emotionally.

CAROLYN: Right, it's unconditional love. You know that person is always there.

COLIN: Now what about when it comes to decision making. There are a lot of big decisions to be made when two people travel the road of life together.

BILL: Oh Colin, that's so important, we call that equality in relationships. When we say equal partners, we don't mean in the legal sense of the word. We mean that their decisions are made jointly. It means that one person makes a decision here, and that's supported; the other person makes a decision there, and that's supported.

CAROLYN: It's like being on a teeter totter, Colin. There's a balance continually, but both people feel that they share their feelings, and they both resolve problems and make decisions. They both feel that they have an equal opportunity to make decisions together. It's not a clinging vine relationship, it's two very independent, strong people coming together and making a strong relationship.

COLIN: Now these two people are having a good relationship. Clearly, this is a happy couple . . .

(laughter)

CAROLYN: That's right.

COLIN: They live together; they spend a lot of time at home. What about when it comes to other activities. Do you find that happy couples do things together?

BILL: Well, we have to recognize the fact that everybody's unique, and everybody has a variety of interests. What they do is they pick out things that they can enjoy together. They have developed common interests, common goals in life.

CAROLYN: Yes, Colin. It may be sports activities or going to shows, or whatever, but they find that out by sharing thoughts and feelings, doing things together develops a feeling of intimacy or closeness. I guess it goes along with the feeling that this is the friend you want to be with, so when you go out to these activities, you have a good time together.

BILL: Exactly. These are the people, Colin, who feel that when they wake up in the morning, and the world seems to be falling apart, there's one thing in your life that seems to be right and good, and that's your partner.

CAROLYN: Yes, that's your partner. You have a good relationship and you don't have to worry about it.

BILL: And those are symptoms of good love.

CAROLYN: Exactly.

COLIN: Yes.

CAROLYN: I guess, also, Colin, that if you're in this sort of relationship seventy to eighty percent of the time, you're really doing well.

BILL: Hang on to a relationship like that. It's a good one.

COLIN: Yes, it sure sounds terrific. Bill and Carolyn, thanks very much.

CAROLYN: Thank you, Colin.

BILL: It was a pleasure, Colin.

QUOTES FROM COUPLES

The best aphrodisiac is an interested and interesting partner.

*One 80-year-old lady said, "In the middle of the afternoon
I lock the doors, pull down the blinds,
and we have a little bit of intercourse.
I tell him it's good for us.
It cleans out the arteries."*

Share *SEX is a 13-Letter Word* with a Friend

Order *Sex is a 13-Letter Word* at $16.95 per book plus $3.50 (total order)
for postage and handling.

SEX is a 13-Letter Word _____ x $16.95 = $ _____

Shipping and handling charge _____ = $ __3.50__

Subtotal _____ = $ _____

In Canada add 7% GST_____(Subtotal x .07) = $ _____

Total enclosed _____ = $ _____

U.S. and international orders payable in U.S. funds/Prices subject to change.

NAME: _____

STREET: _____

CITY: _____ PROV./STATE _____

COUNTRY _____ POSTAL CODE/ZIP _____

Please make cheque or money order payable to: **Verbal Dance Publications
502 Queen Street
Saskatoon, Saskatchewan
Canada S7K 0M5**

For fund raising or volume purchase prices, contact **Verbal Dance Publications**.

Share *SEX is a 13-Letter Word* with a Friend

Order *Sex is a 13-Letter Word* at $16.95 per book plus $3.50 (total order)
for postage and handling.

SEX is a 13-Letter Word _____ x $16.95 = $ _____

Shipping and handling charge _____ = $ __3.50__

Subtotal _____ = $ _____

In Canada add 7% GST_____(Subtotal x .07) = $ _____

Total enclosed _____ = $ _____

U.S. and international orders payable in U.S. funds/Prices subject to change.

NAME: _____

STREET: _____

CITY: _____ PROV./STATE _____

COUNTRY _____ POSTAL CODE/ZIP _____

Please make cheque or money order payable to: **Verbal Dance Publications
502 Queen Street
Saskatoon, Saskatchewan
Canada S7K 0M5**

For fund raising or volume purchase prices, contact **Verbal Dance Publications**.